Midland Ontario Book 1 in Colour Photos, Saving Our History One Photo at a Time

Photography
by Barbara Raué
2016

Series Name: Cruising Ontario

Book 150: Midland Book 1

Cover photo: 414 King Street, Page 32

Series Name: Cruising Ontario
Saving Our History One Photo at a Time
in colour photos

Books Available in Alphabetical Order:
Aberfoyle, Acton, Alton, Amherstburg, Ancaster, Arthur, Aylmer, Ayr, Bloomingdale, Brantford, Burlington, Caledon, Caledonia, Cambridge, Clifford, Conestogo, Delhi, Dorchester to Aylmer, Drayton, Drumbo, Dundas, Eden Mills, Elmira, Elora, Essex, Fergus, Guelph, Hagersville, Hamilton, Hanover, Harriston, Hespeler, Jarvis, Kingston, Kingsville, Kitchener, Linwood, Listowel, London, Lucknow, Mono, Mount Forest, Neustadt, New Hamburg, Niagara-on-the-Lake, Oakville, Orangeville, Orillia, Owen Sound, Palmerston, Peterborough, Petrolia, Port Elgin, Preston, Rockwood, Sarnia, Seaforth, Sheffield, Shelburne, Simcoe, Southampton, St. Jacobs, St. Marys, St. Thomas, Stoney Creek, Stratford, Thamesford, Tillsonburg, Waterdown, Waterford, Waterloo, Welland, Wellesley, Windsor, Wingham, Woodstock

Book 123-124: Kingsville
Book 125-127: Woodstock
Book 128: Thamesford
Book 129-132: St. Marys
Book 133-136: Sarnia
Book 137: Petrolia
Book 138-139: Welland
Book 140-145: Kingston
Book 146-149: Ottawa
Book 150-151: Midland

Other Books by Barbara Raue

Coins of Gold

Arrows, Indians and Love

The Life and Times of Barbara
Volume 1: Inventions That Have Enhanced My Life
Volume 2: Entertainment That I Have Enjoyed
Volume 3: East Coast Trips
Volume 4: Olympics Have Always Intrigued Me
Volume 5: Wonders of the World
Volume 6: Caribbean Cruises We Have Enjoyed
Volume 7: Animals
Volume 8: Storms and Other Major Disasters in My Lifetime
Volume 9: Wars, Terrorist Attacks and Major Disasters

The Cromwell Family Book

Laura Secord Discovered

Daddy Where Are You?

Montana Series
Book 1: Montana Dream
Book 2: Life on the Montana Frontier
Book 3: Montana to Boston and Back

Visit Barbara's website to view all of her books
http://barbararaue.ca

Table of Contents

Midland is located on the southern end of Georgian Bay's 30,000 Islands about ninety miles north of Toronto.

Huronia was named for the Huron Nation and consists of the areas around southeastern Georgian Bay which include Midland and Penetanguishene. The area was visited by French Jesuits traveling with the Voyageurs to the Wye River in 1639. They were welcomed by the Huron tribe who traded furs and skins for metal goods and clothing from France. They built a settlement named Fort Ste. Marie which thrived for ten years until it was burned to the ground in 1649 by the Jesuits themselves after repeated attacks from Iroquois who were in league with the English who wanted the French share of the fur trade in North America. Some of the priests were martyred. The Sainte-Marie among the Hurons site was discovered in 1947, excavated and rebuilt to its original form by archeologists from the University of Western Ontario.

The Jesuits attempted a second site on St. Joseph's Island, currently Christian Island, and named it Sainte Marie II. They carried many of their goods by raft to this second site. After a winter of terrible hardship and starvation, the Jesuits decided to abandon their mission and returned to Quebec in 1650. Christian Island was later declared a native reservation by the Canadian government.

In 1871 a group of the principal shareholders of the Midland Railway, headed by Adolph Hugel, chose this location as the northern terminus of their line which they ran from Port Hope to Beaverton. The town site was surveyed in 1872-73. The railway line was completed in 1879 and soon attracted settlers to the area. The new community, Midland, achieved its early growth through shipping and the lumber and grain trade.

In and around the center of Midland there are a number of murals most of which were painted by now deceased artist Fred Lenz.

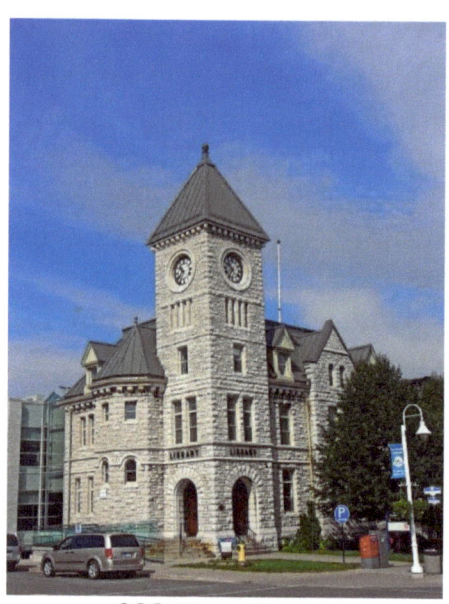
320 King Street

The impressive Romanesque style limestone structure which now houses the library was built in 1913 as Midland's first post office, with customs and excise offices on the second floor. - mansard roof, high central gable, imposing corner porch, and tower; 2½ storey building composed of even course cut stone, with a belt course that goes around the entire building; metal roof has a decorative stone fascia; some semi-elliptical windows, and a corner entrance.

In 1963 the post office, needing more space, moved to its new home on Dominion Avenue and the beautiful limestone building sat empty for three years. In 1967, the library moved to the old post office.

Setting your watch by the clock tower would be inadvisable as the four faces do not always agree.

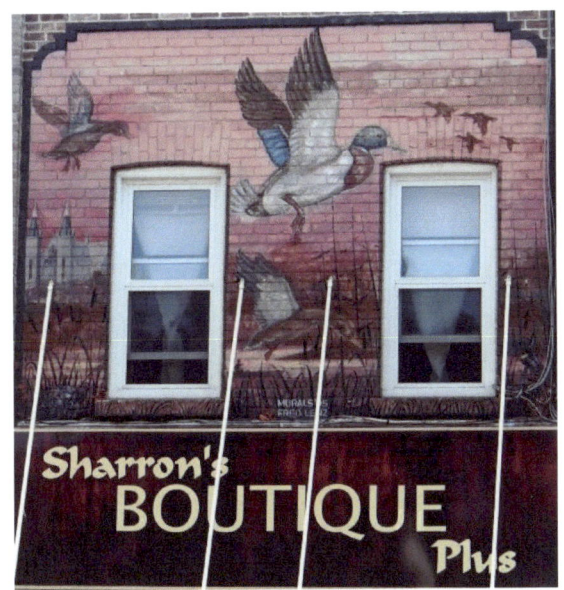

The Wye Marsh Mural

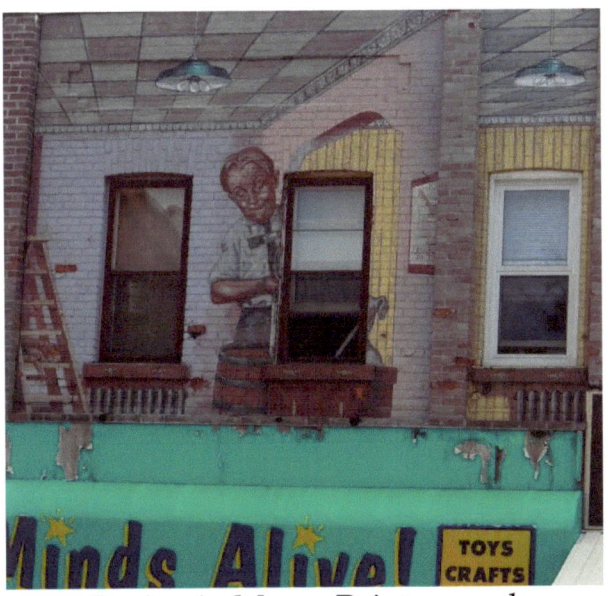

Benjamin Moore Paints mural

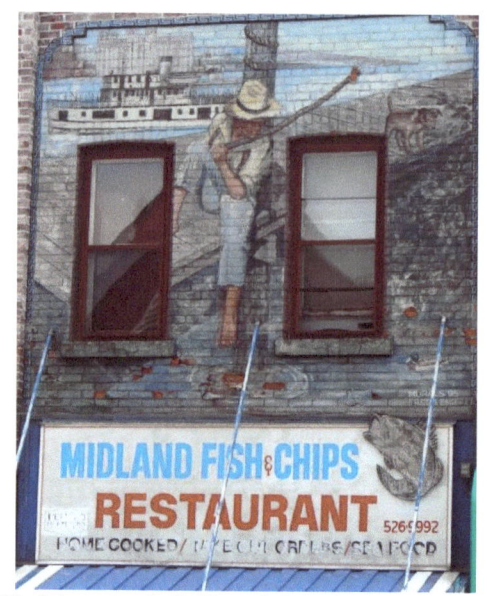

Fishing in Midland Harbour mural

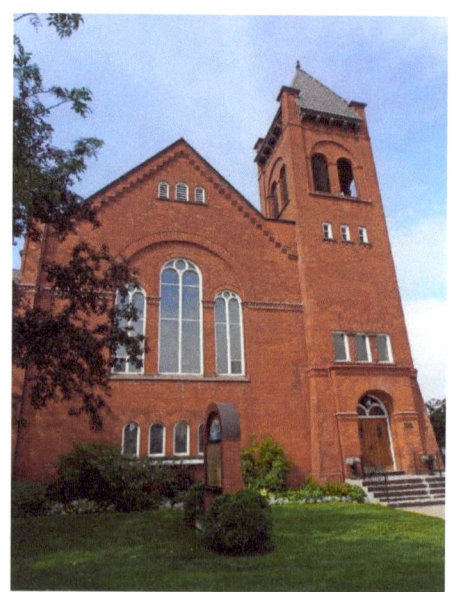

308 King Street - St. Paul's United Church – 1897 –
Romanesque – dentil molding, banding, bell tower

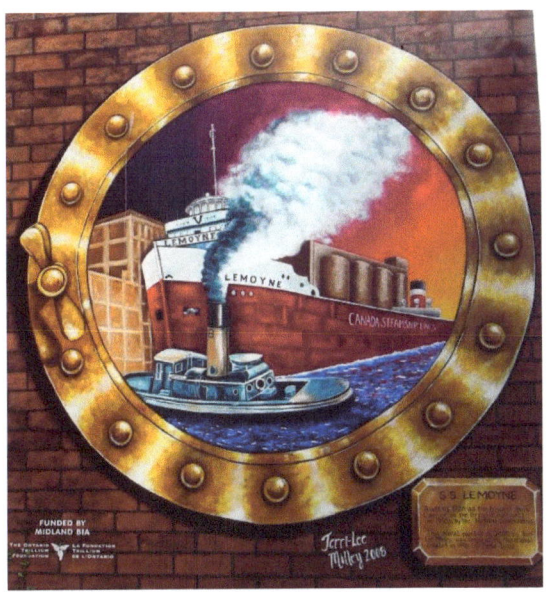

S. S. Lemoyne mural – built in 1926 by the Midland Shipbuilding Company - the largest Bulk Carrier on the Great Lakes until the 1950s. This mural, painted in 2008 by Terri-Lee Milley, was inspired by the original created in 1996 by Fred Lenz.

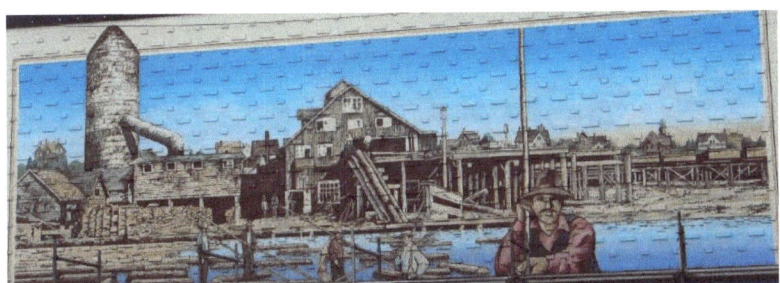

Playfair Lumber Mill in 1890 mural - the first lumber mill in Midland

Mural located at corner of Hugel Avenue and Bourgeois Lane

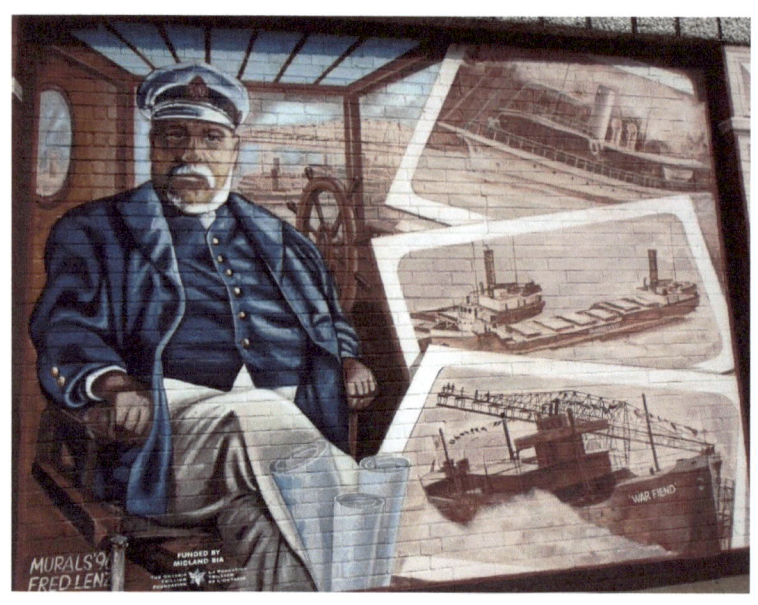

James Playfair Shipyard mural shows the late James Playfair. He had a large impact on the growth of Midland. He was a successful Midland lumberman owning lumberyards, and he turned to shipping in 1896. In 1901 he formed the Midland Navigation Company; in 1910 he formed the Midland Dry Dock Company, which he re-named in 1915 the Midland Shipbuilding Company to build ocean ships for World War I. He was co-owner of a general store in the early 1900s. In 1917, James Playfair's company completed a large new shipyard on the Midland waterfront to build government contracted Ocean Cargo Steamers. The first one launched was the "War Fiend" (1918). In 1920 he started the Great Lakes Transportation Company and the "The Glen Line".

Mural located on the north/east side of Hugel Avenue

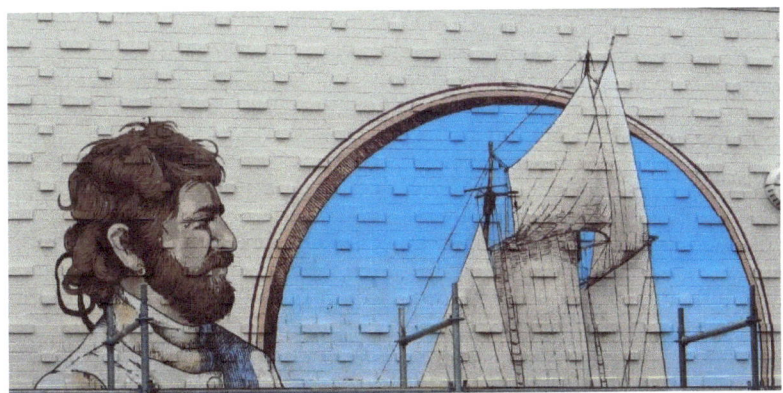

H. M. Schooner Bee - The original Bee sailed Georgian Bay from 1871 to 1931. A replica has been made and is docked in Penetanguishene Harbour at Discovery Harbour.
Mural located at the corner of King Street and Hugel Avenue

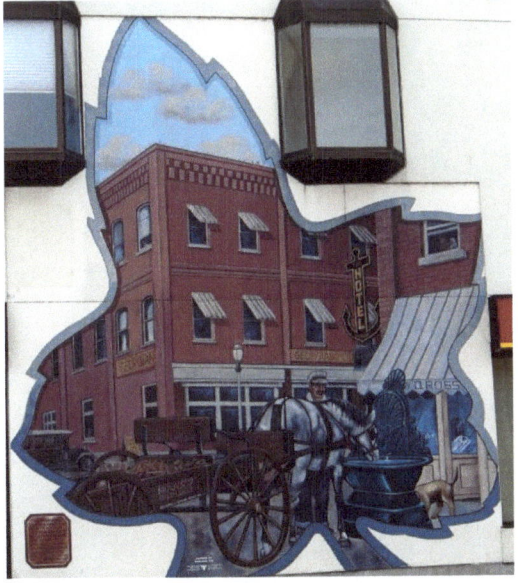

The Water Fountain mural - This painting represents the same corner as it would have looked like in the 1920s. The water fountain was a place you and your horse could stop to take a drink.
Mural located on south/west corner of Hugel Avenue and King Street

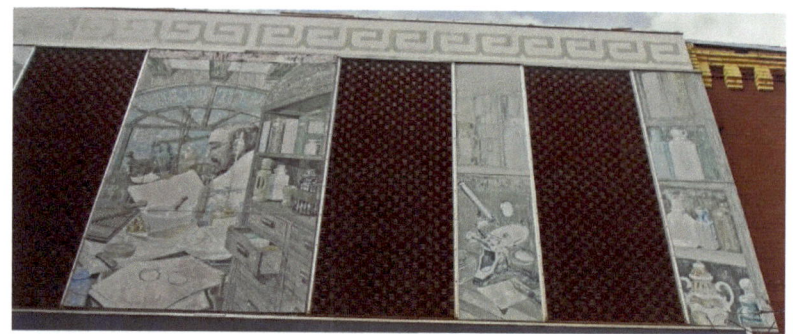

Druggist mural - On the second floor of this building is a view into an apothecary shop. The gentleman in the mural is one of many druggists who acted as a chemist by mixing their own cures as outlined by the physician.

Mural located on King Street, north of Hugel Avenue

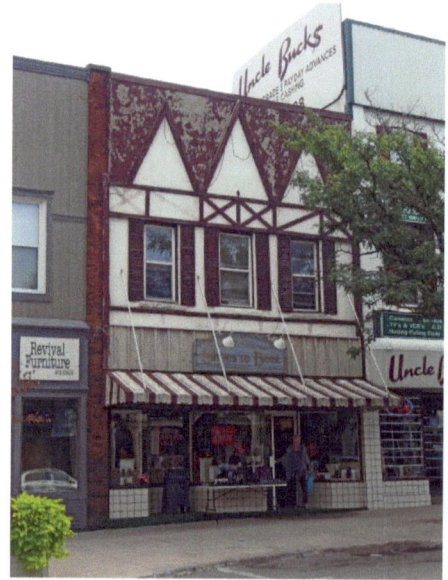

261 King Street – Shoes to Boot

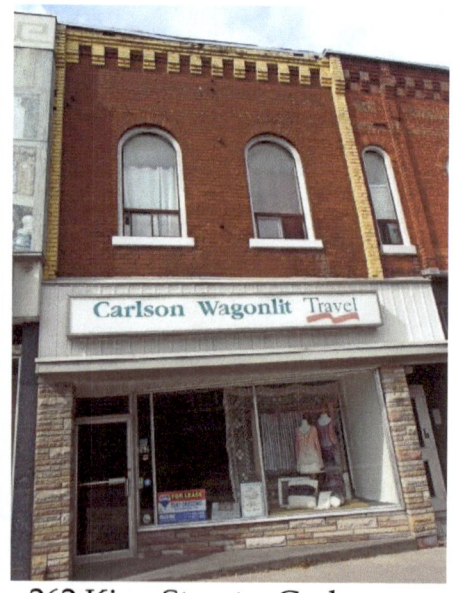

262 King Street – Carlson Wagonlit Travel – dentil moulding, voussoirs

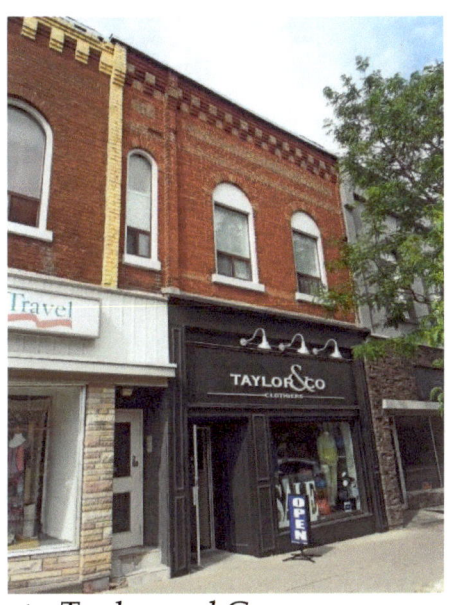

260 King Street - Taylor and Company – men's clothing –
dentil molding, voussoirs, dichromatic brickwork

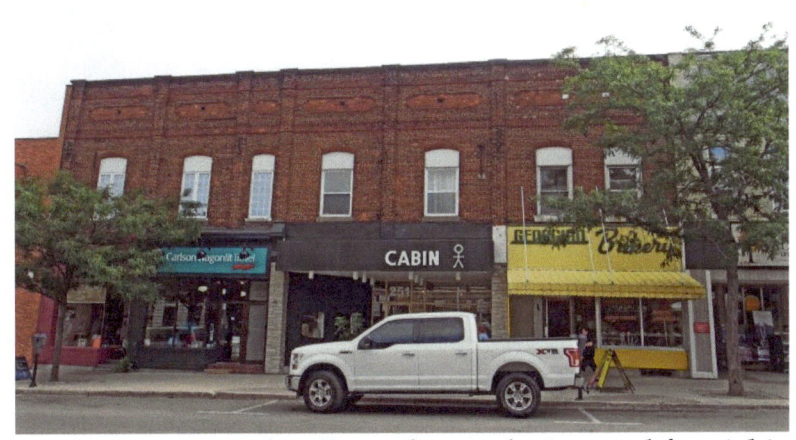

251 King Street – Cabin Boy – home design and furnishings
253 King Street – Georgian Bakery
Pilasters

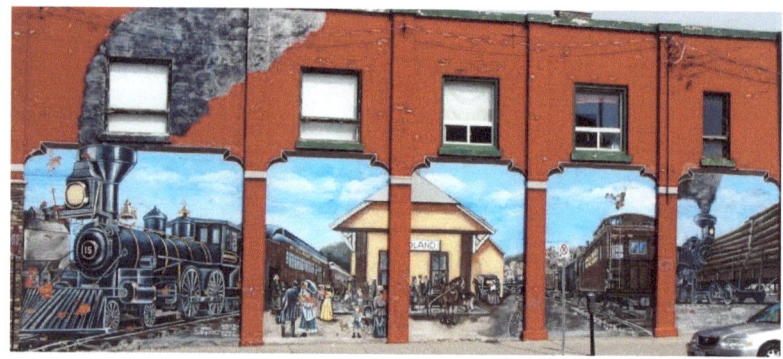

Midland Railway Corporation - This mural shows the engine house. The men working are repositioning the turntable to allow the locomotive to exit the yard.

Mural located on Dominion Avenue

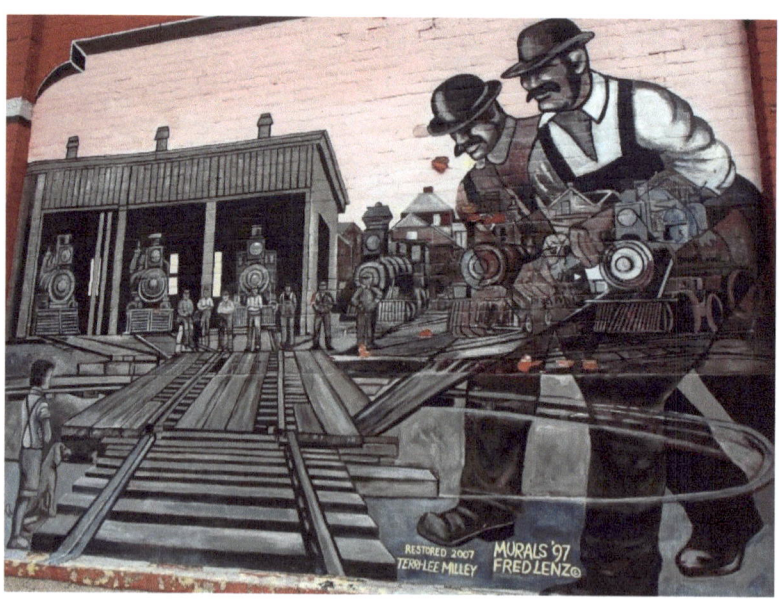

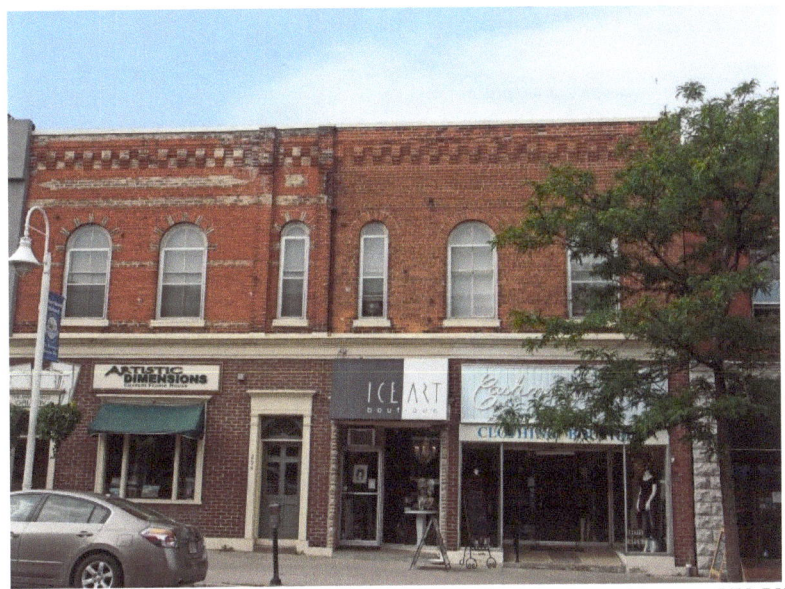

254 King Street – Artistic Dimensions – Custom Frame House; 252 King Street – Ice Art; 250 King Street – Cashmere Blue Clothing Boutique

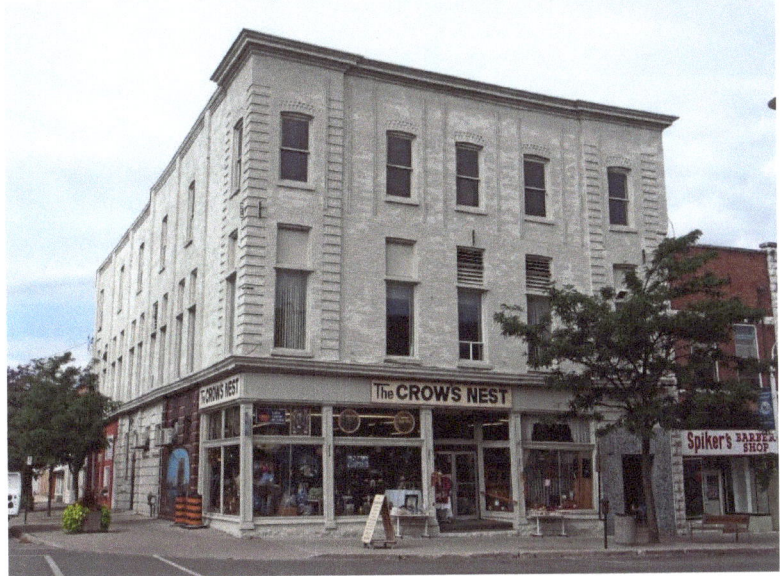

234-236 King Street - Jeffery Block – 1901 – Romanesque Revival style - large number and regular rhythm of windows; extend brick corner quoins and varied brick courses on the window lintels - The Crow's Nest Pub and Restaurant is now where the hardware store was; second floor YMCA; top floor Odd Fellows lodge meeting rooms

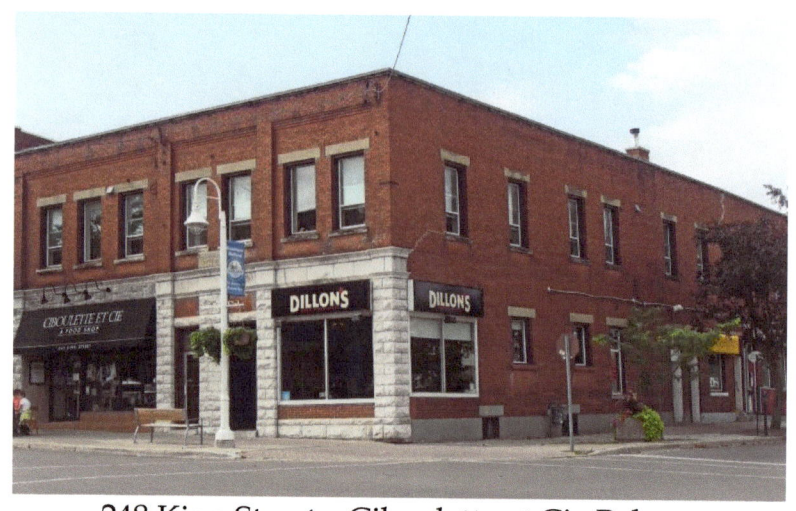

248 King Street – Ciboulette et Cie Bakery
244 King Street - Dillons – wood fired pizza
Ingram Block - 1914

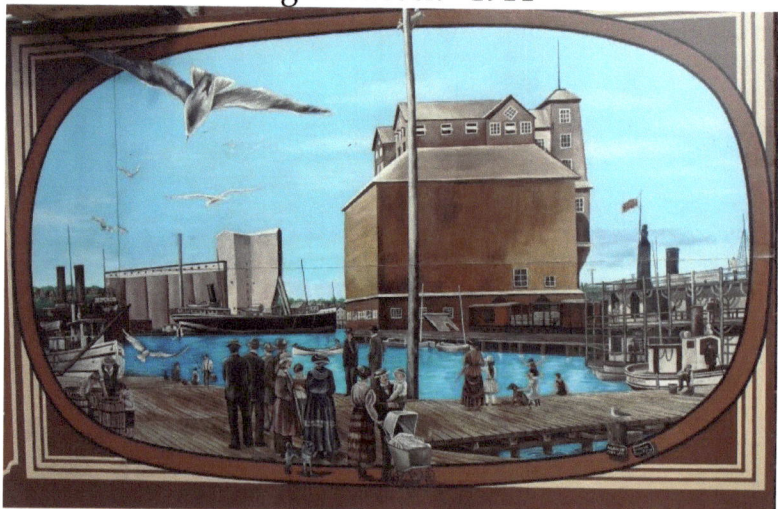

View of Midland Harbour early 1900s - Based on a photograph taken by J.W Bald in the early 1900s. It reveals how much the lives of the local residents centred on the Midland Harbour. Since Midland was situated at the southern end of Georgian Bay it was predicted that Midland would become the "Chicago of the North".

Located at the corner of King Street and Dominion Avenue

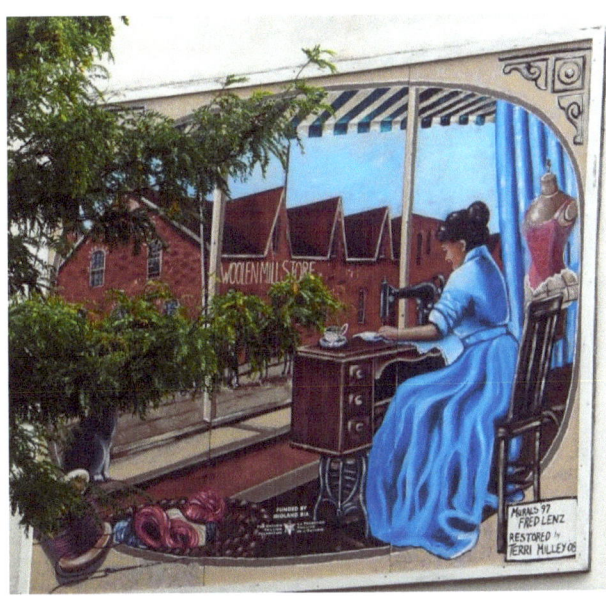

Woolen Mill - In this mural you see a woman working on an early model sewing machine while her cat stares out the window across the road at the Woolen Mill Store.

Located on King Street, north of Dominion Avenue

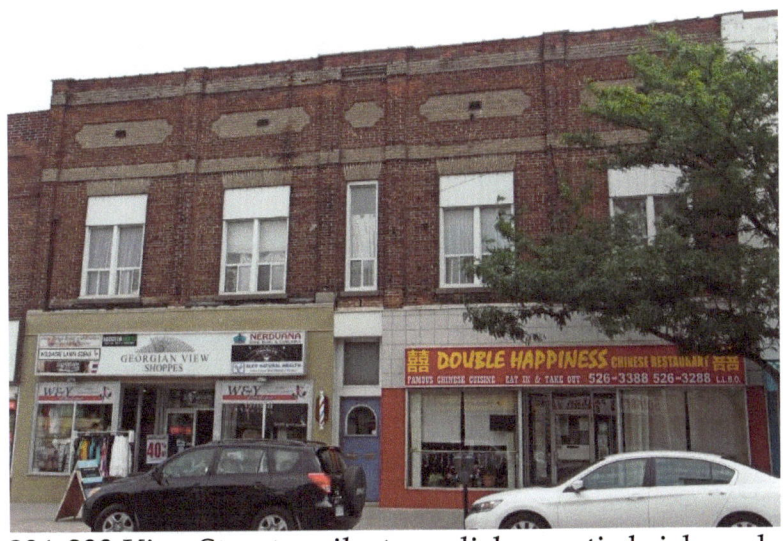

231-233 King Street – pilasters, dichromatic brickwork, voussoirs

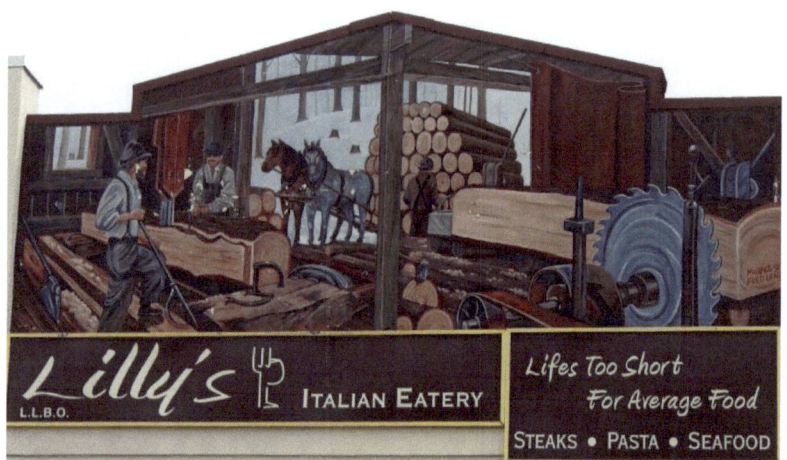

Saw Mill - This mural displays what a typical saw mill looked like in the 1900s. The lumber industry played a major role in the growth of Midland and the surrounding areas.

Mural located at bottom of King Street on a store front

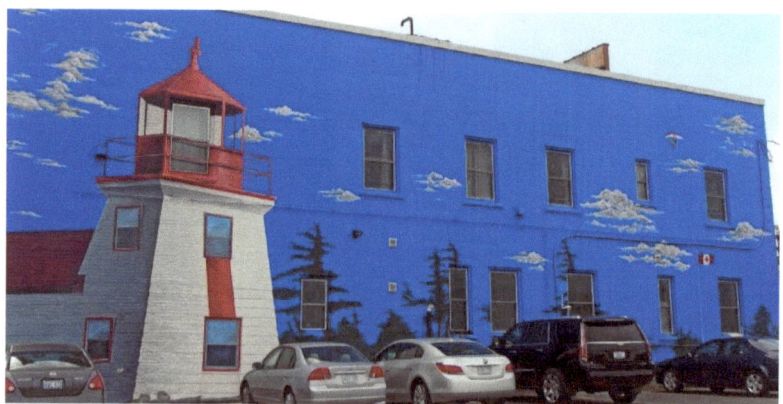

Brebeuf Lighthouse mural - This lighthouse was built in the 1900s to help guide ships on course from Giant's Tomb to the channel serving Midland Bay. The window in the top of the lighthouse is real.

Mural located at the corner of King Street and Bay Street

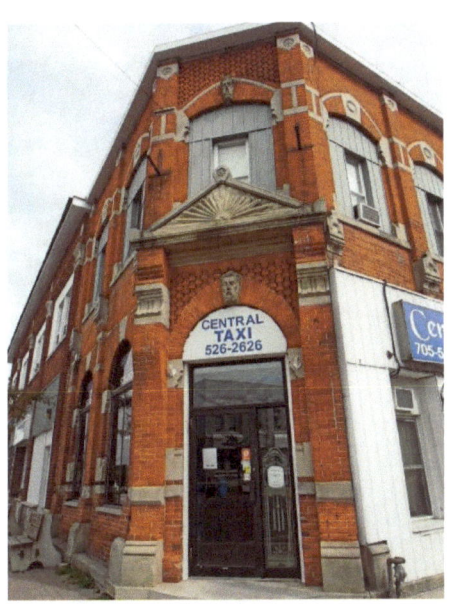

203-207 King Street - two storey, flat roofed commercial building - Burton Block, built by the Burton Brothers of Barrie - exterior of the building is made up of board and batten, stretcher brick, poured concrete, and sheet metal siding; frontispiece and decorated panels; brick keystones above windows; blind transom above door

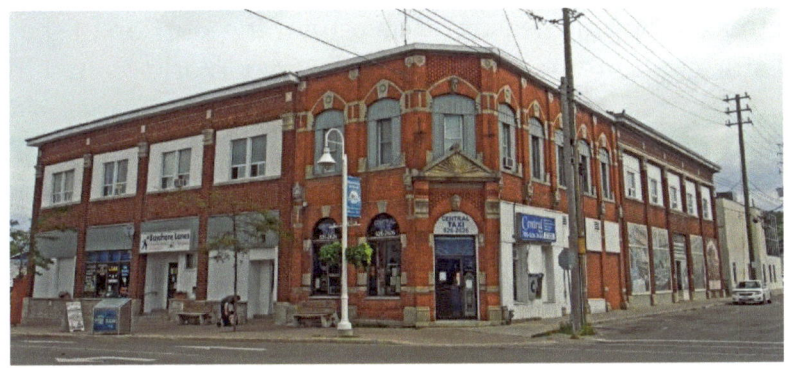

The original stone carvings of Greek gods are still intact above the Taxi Stand door.

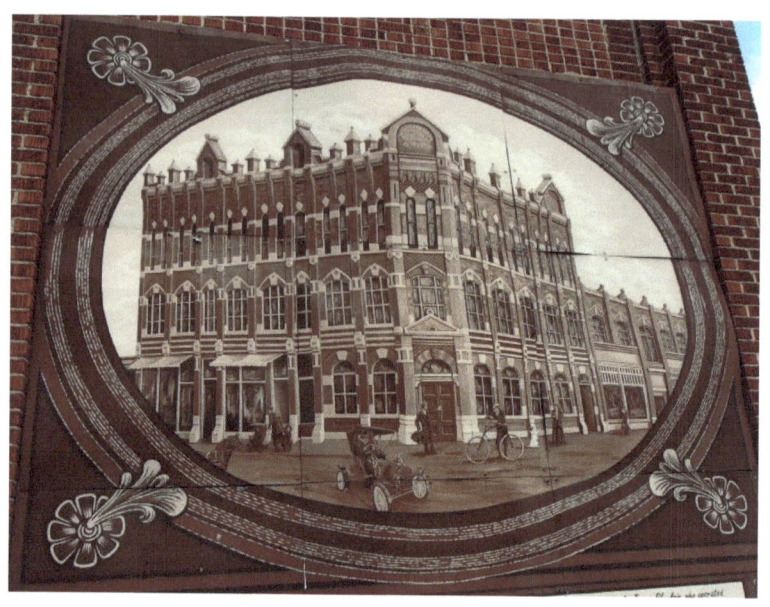

Western Bank of Canada built Midland's first bank in 1882. In 1895 the building was sold to William Preston and James Playfair who operated a general department store and wholesale business until the sale of the property in the 1950s. A portion of the third storey collapsed in 1928 during a busy Christmas shopping season. The remaining portion of the third storey was removed after the Second World War. Other businesses operating from this location over the years included Eaton's (the largest department store north of Toronto), the Unemployment Insurance Commission, Dance Halls, and an I.G.A. grocery store. The present Bowling Centre and Taxi Stand have been in existence since 1948. The only original superstructure remaining is located at the southwest corner of the building.

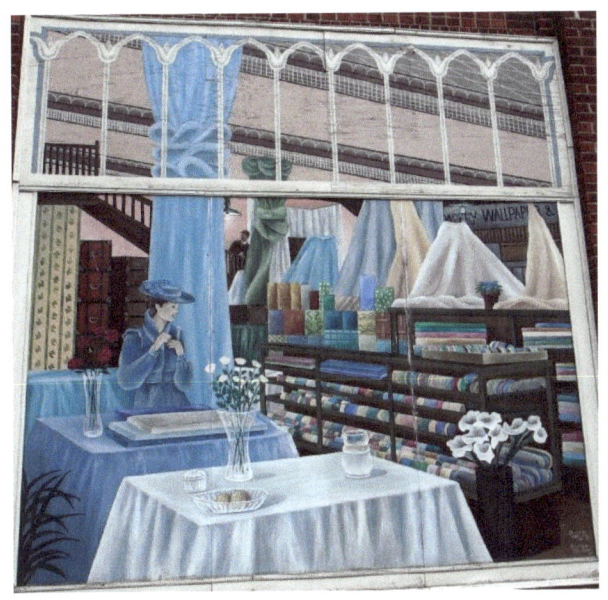

The Playfair Preston Company mural - This general store was in operation from 1895 to 1950s - Mural located on Bay Street between Midland Avenue and King Street

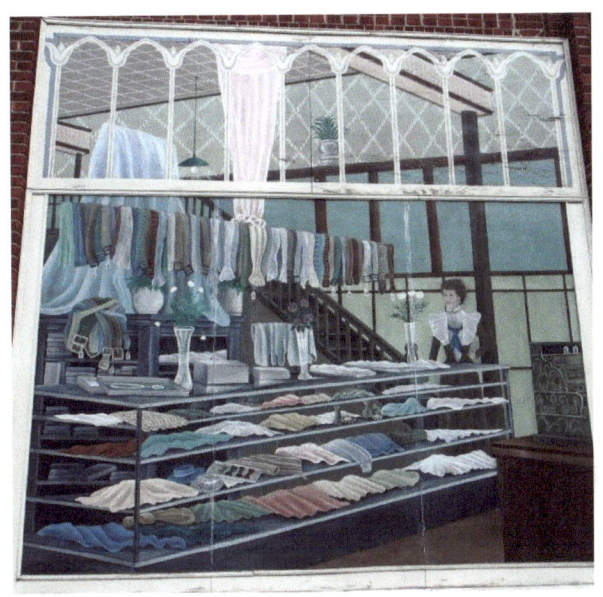

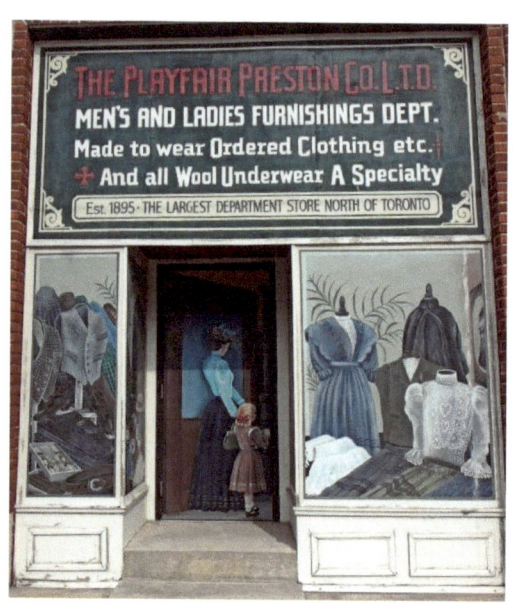

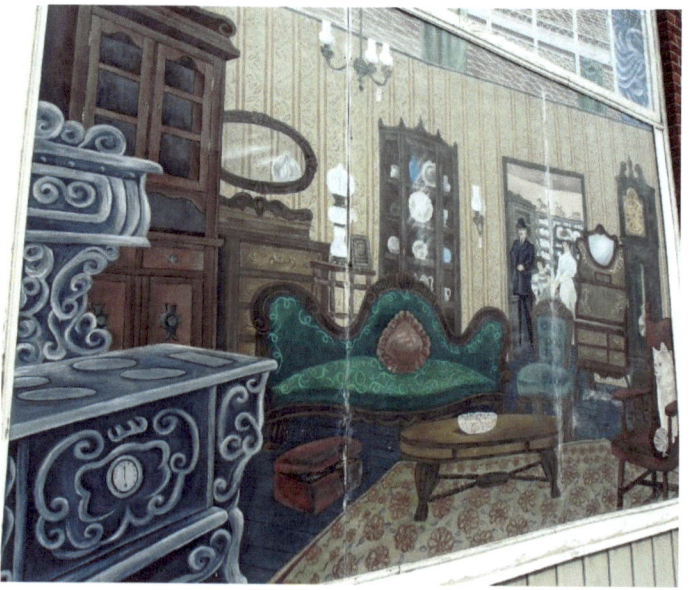

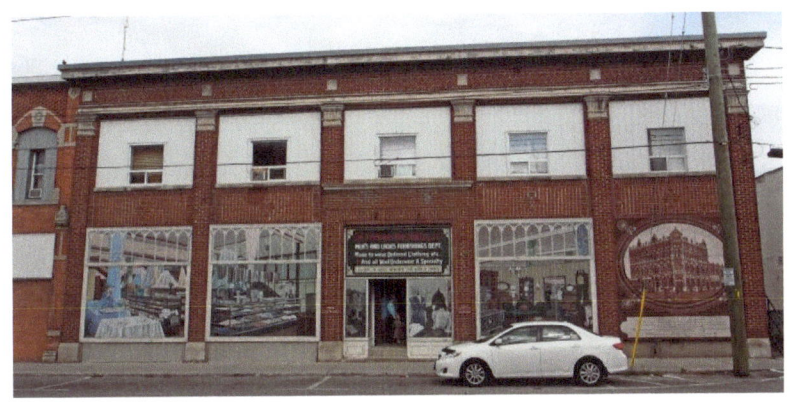

Mural located on Bay Street between Midland Avenue and King Street

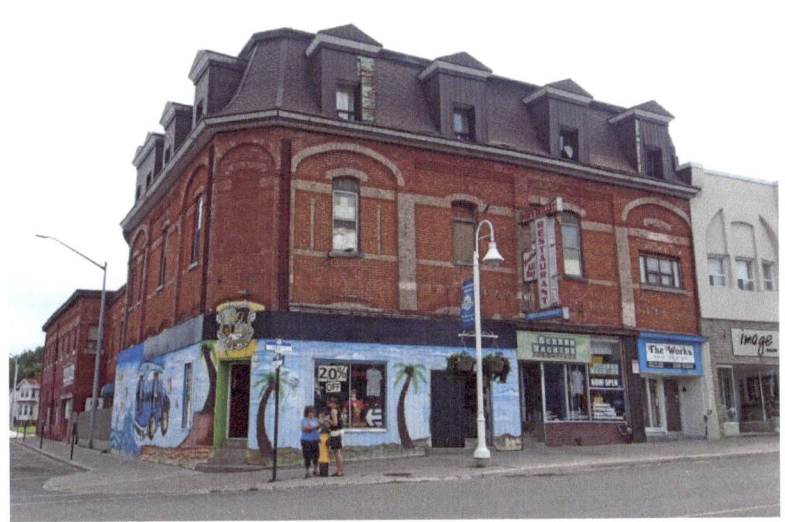

213-219 King Street – Second Empire – mansard roof, dormers, dichromatic brickwork

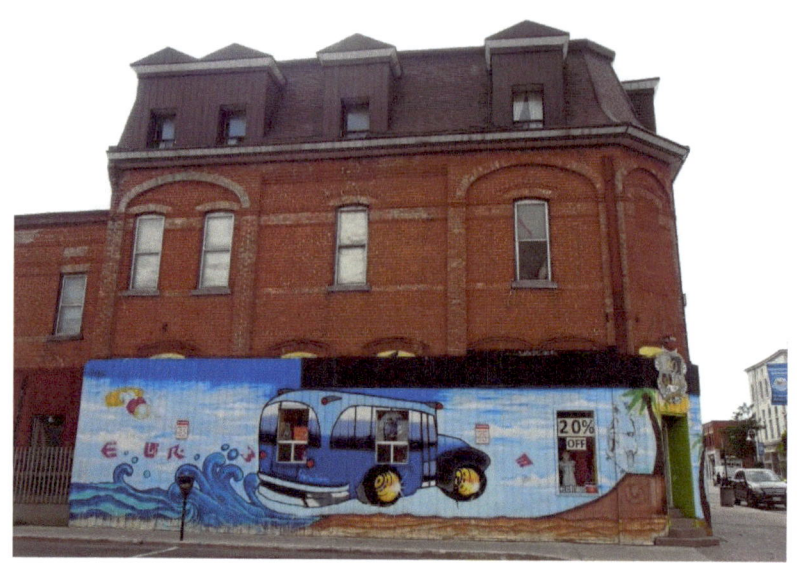

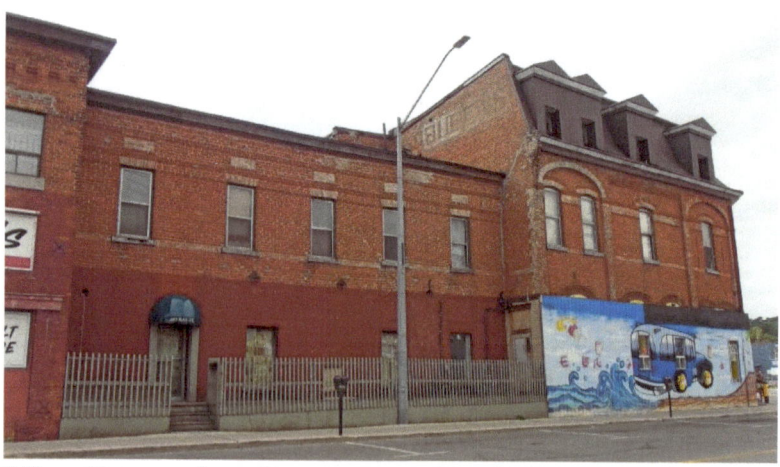

486 Bay Street – banding, voussoirs, dichromatic brickwork

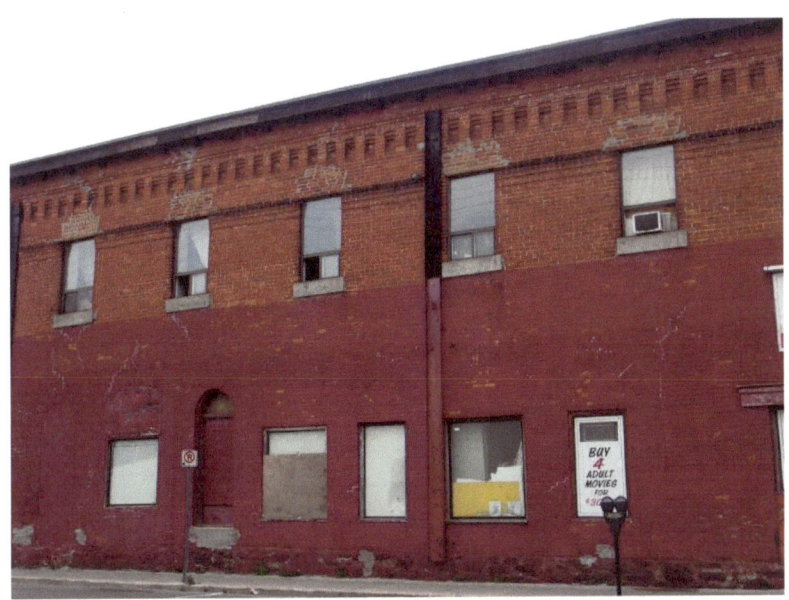

486 Bay Street – dentil moulding

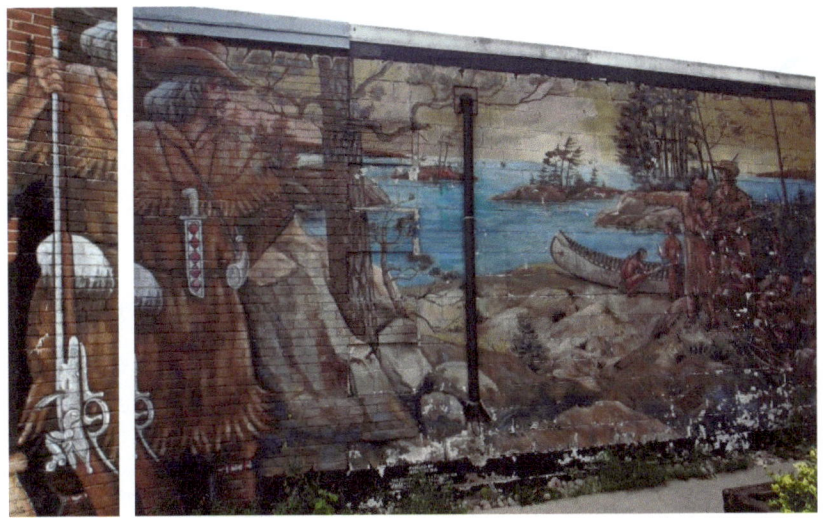

Runner of the Woods - This mural shows fur traders (left)
meeting and working with the Hurons (right). The rocks are
similar to those in the Canadian Shield.

Mural located at the bottom of King Street

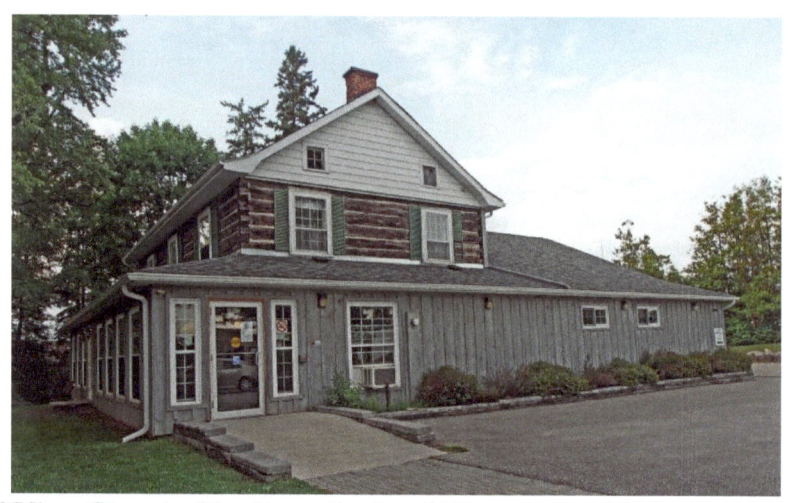

687 King Street - Heritage Animal Hospital – 1900 – exterior is board and batten, clap board, and horizontal finished log; sidelights

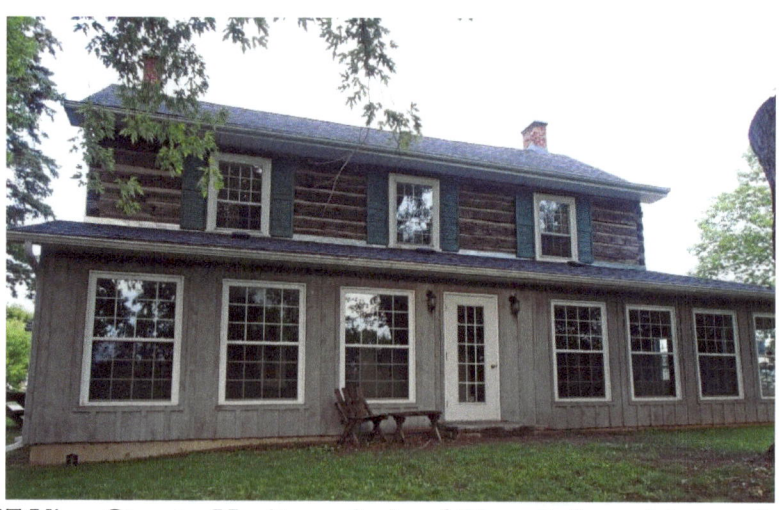

687 King Street - Heritage Animal Hospital - a skirt roof on three sides, with a medium gabled roof and a medium hipped roof; 12- over- 12 paned windows

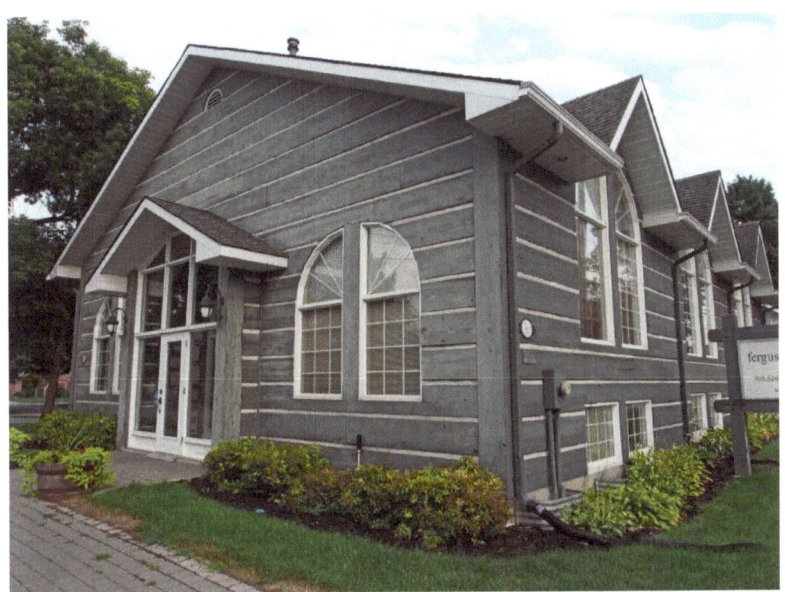

531 King Street – 1½ storeys with a full basement; low gable roof with a double gable on the façade with a molded fascia; exterior is finished with log; windows have a quarter-circle opening with molded trim inside the opening; 6-over-6 pane arrangement; main entrance has an ogee shaped opening with a plain pediment roof above and wood piers on the sides; windows above the door and sidelights beside

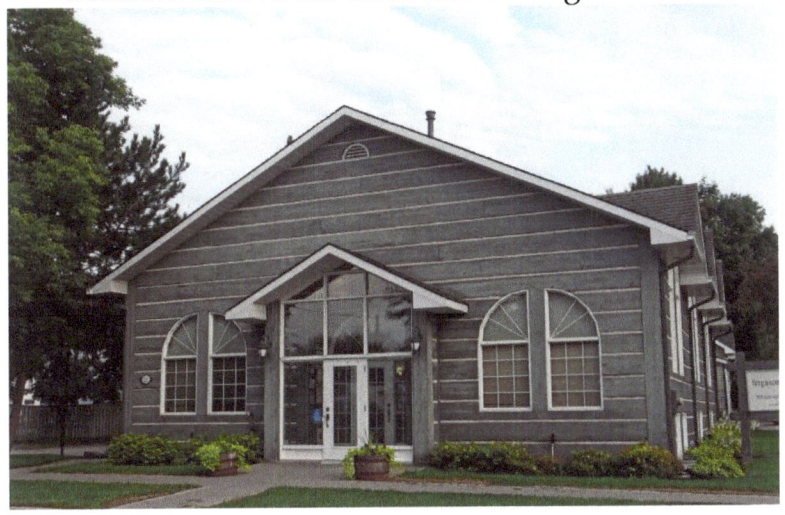

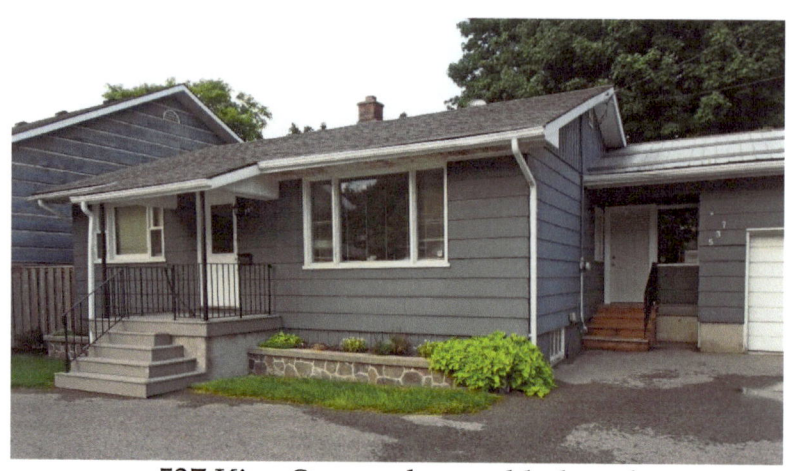

537 King Street – low-gabled roof

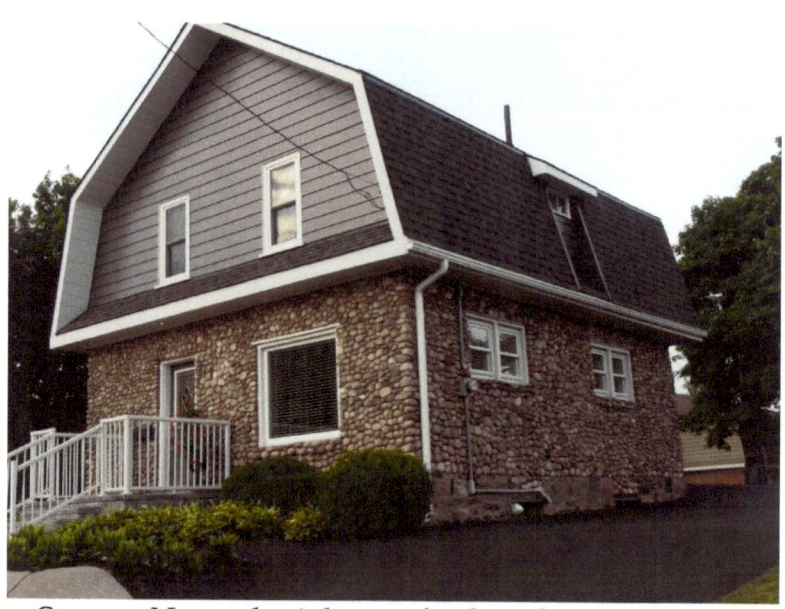

King Street – Neo-colonial - gambrel roof; exterior is finished
with field stone; cobblestone basement

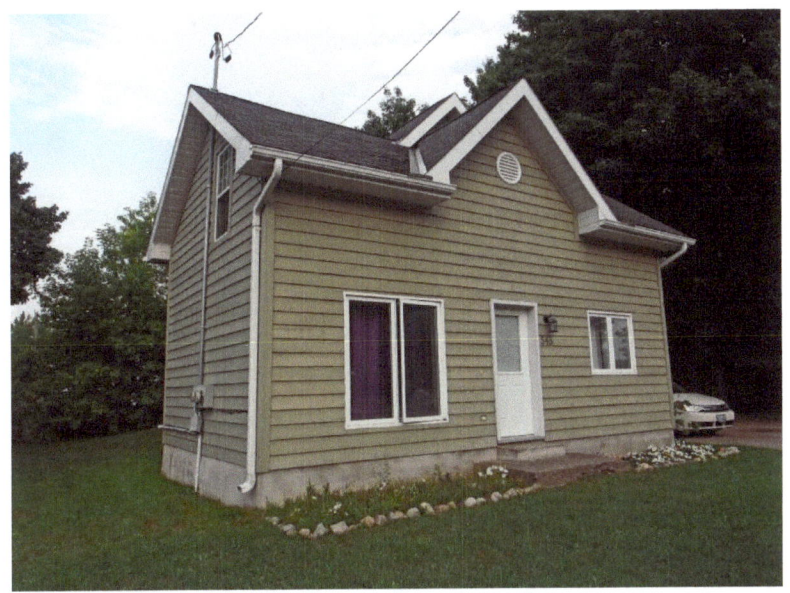

543 King Street – Gothic

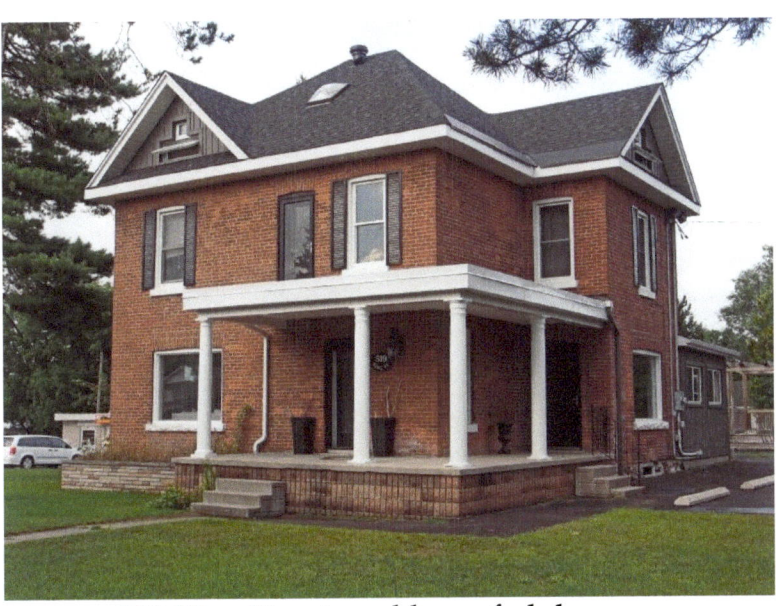

519 King Street - gable roofed dormers

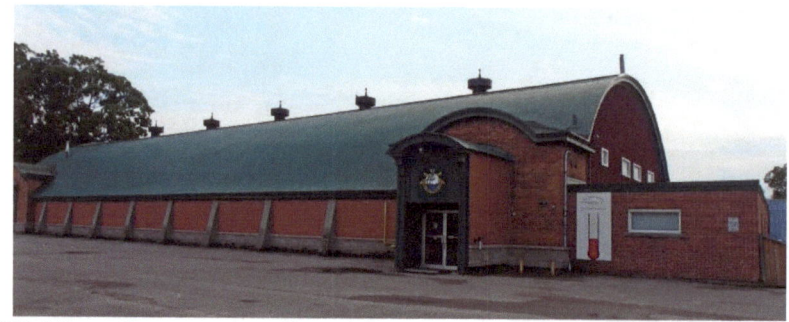

472 King Street – Midland Curling Club – 1919 – Italianate styled entrance - long rectangular façade; exterior is brick, poured concrete and metal; dome roof covered with steel; small flat roofed area

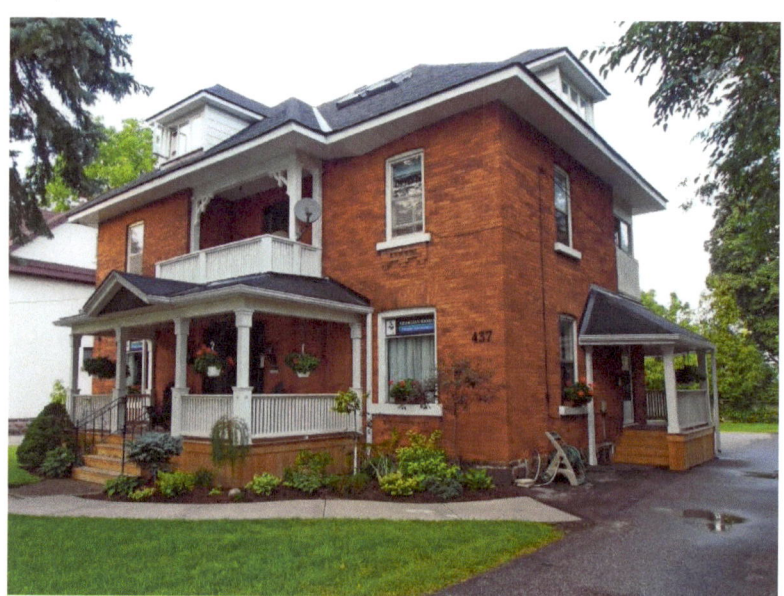

437 King Street - exterior is stretcher brick with a cut stone foundation; medium hipped roof and two second storey balconies; brick voussoirs; decorative brick below some windows; sidelights; open verandah with open railings and wood piers

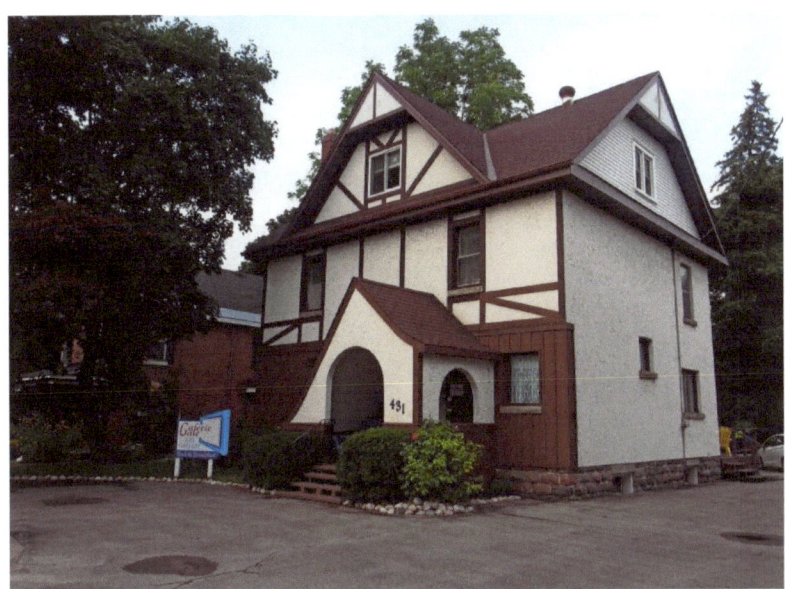

431 King Street - full basement; low gable roof with a double gable on the façade with a molded fascia; exterior is finished with log; main entrance has an ogee shaped opening with a plain pediment roof above and wood piers on sides

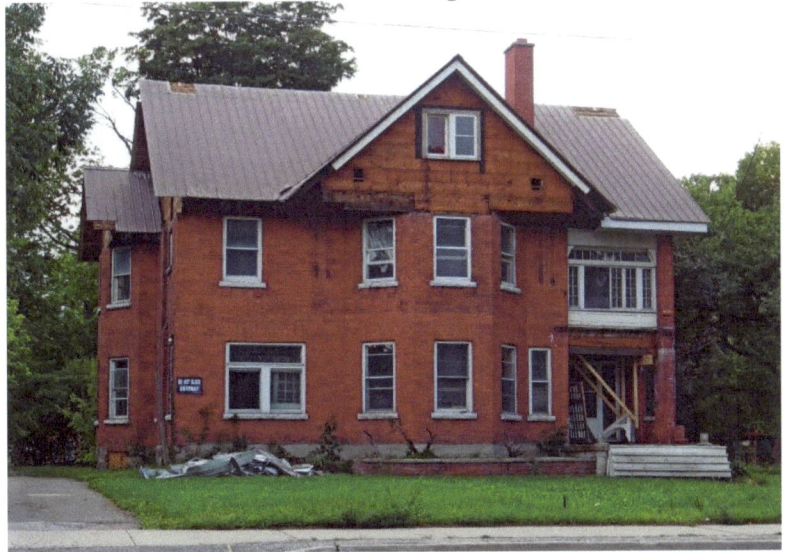

422 King Street – 2½ storey house has a gabled roof with a center gable; large knee-wall structure supporting the steel roof; stained glass fanlight above window on left side; sidelights – under repair

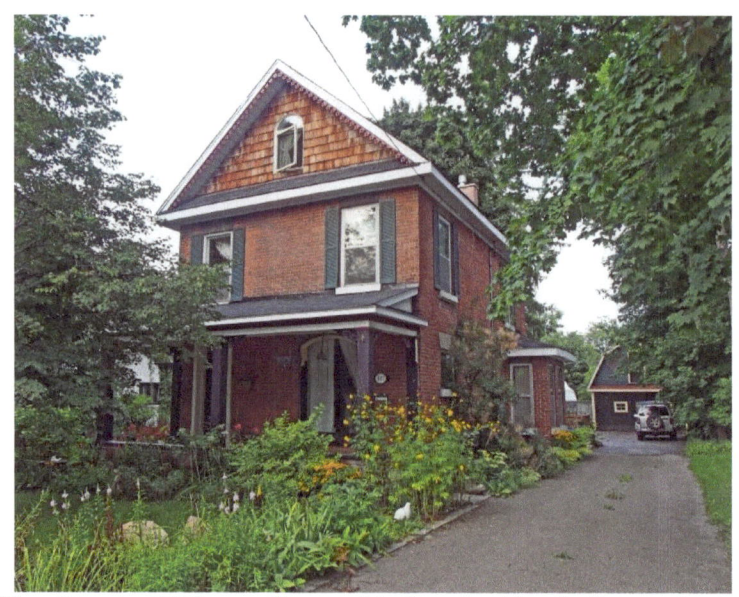

427 King Street – 1902 - medium gabled roof with a half-round window; gingerbread trim on fascia; exterior is cedar shingles and stretcher brick; brick voussoirs and window shutters; transom window

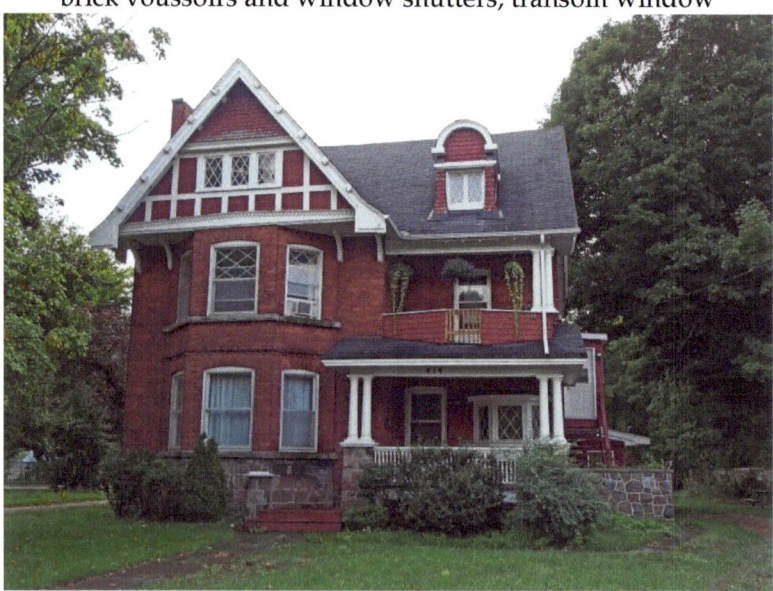

414 King Street – late 1800s - 2½ storey brick, Gothic Revival - dichromatic brick patterns, roof gables and dormer with rounded roof, various window shapes and sizes, mixed design verge boards and verandas

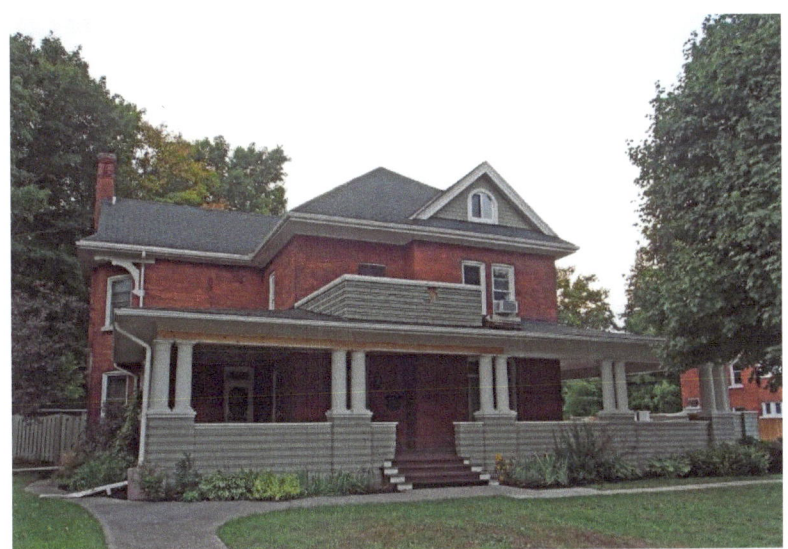

408 King Street – 1912 - Jory House - square house with a wing on front, back and left side; exterior is stretcher brick, wood shingles, and terra cotta; upper storey door to a closed railing balcony; front wing has a medium hipped roof while the left wing has a gambrel roof; gable roofed dormer with semi-elliptical window; transom above door; open verandah with closed railing and wood pedestals with Doric capital columns

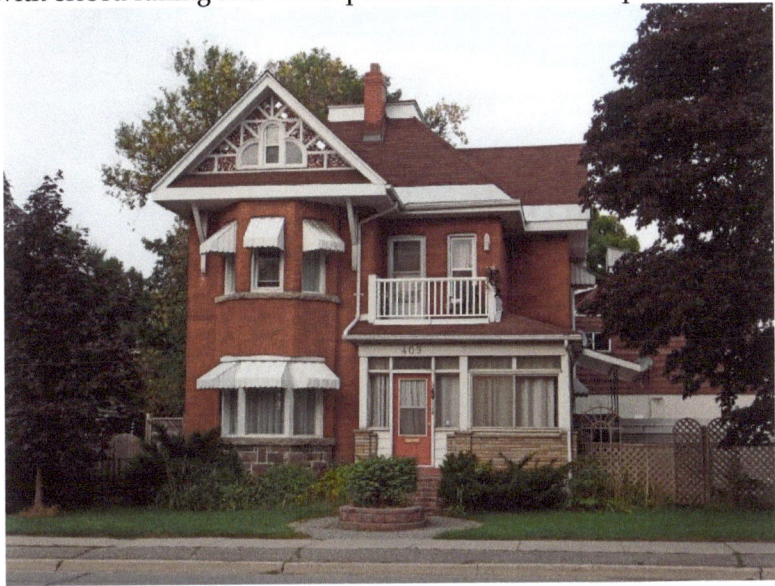

409 King Street – Palladian window in gable roofed dormer; two-storey bay window; second floor balcony above closed in porch; varied roofline

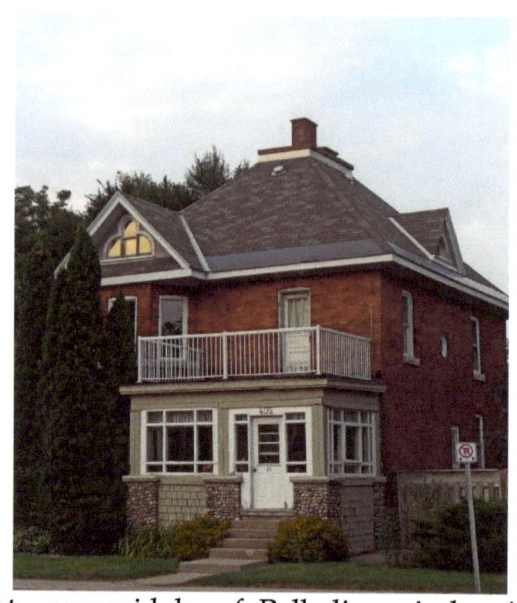

405 King Street – pyramidal roof; Palladian window in gable roofed dormers; two-storey bay window; second floor balcony above closed in porch

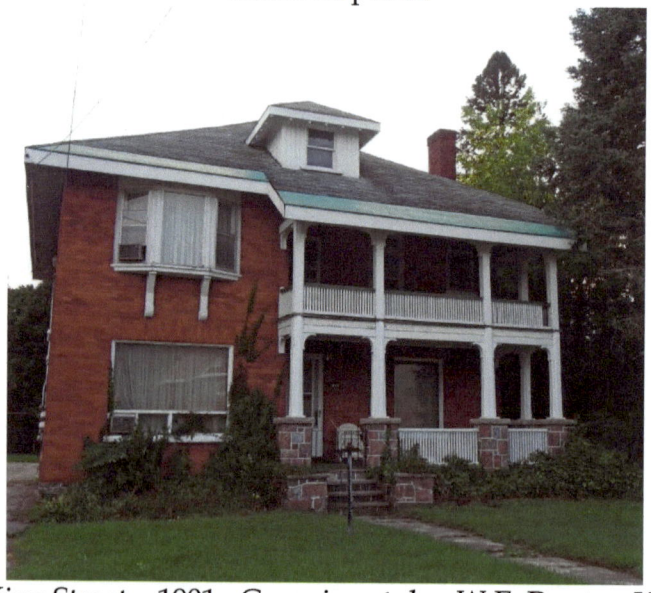

400 King Street – 1901 - Georgian style - W.E. Preston House (worked as clerk in James Freeborn's general store) - columns and corresponding porch on second storey; hipped roof; dormer

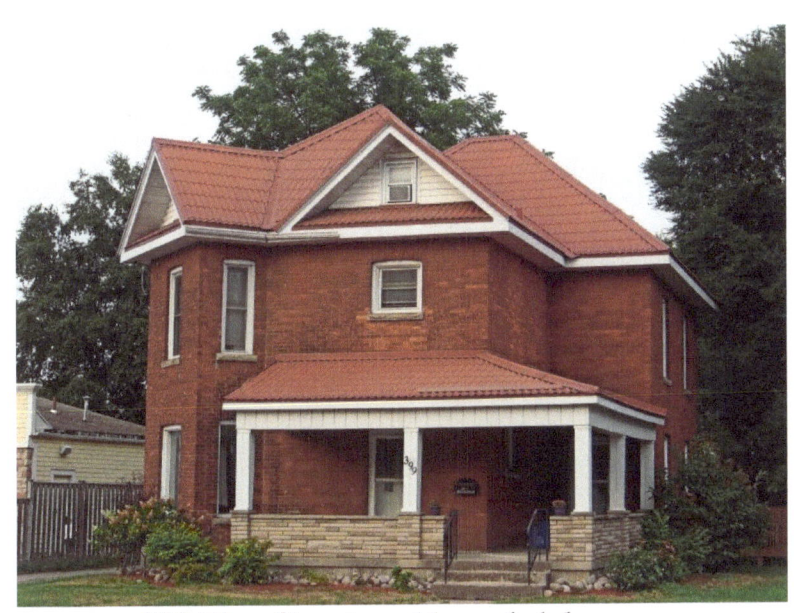

399 King Street - gable roofed dormers

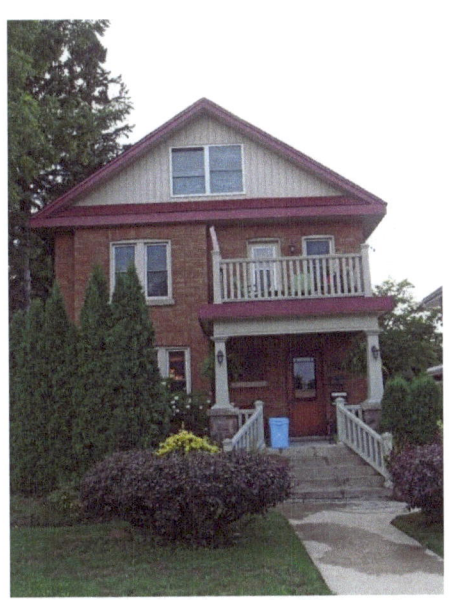

394 King Street - exterior is brick and board and batten; gabled roof with a cross gable on the side; brick voussoirs; second storey balcony above porch

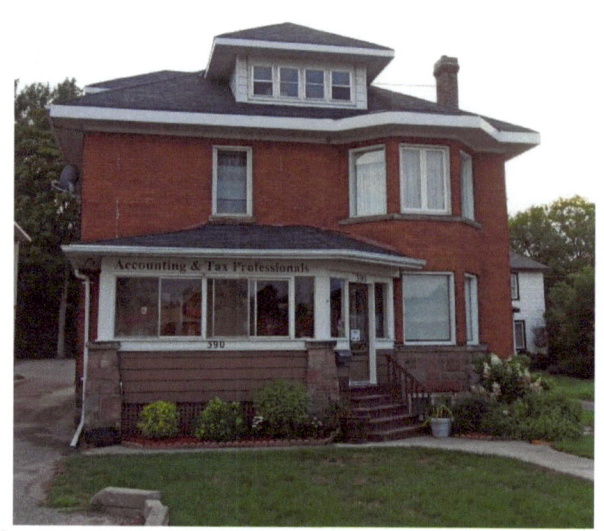

390 King Street – 1910 - Keller House (once owned by Mr. M. Seymour Keller, a business owner) - soldier course brick voussoirs over windows; multi-level pyramidal roof; hipped roof dormer and a small bay dormer; two-storey bay window

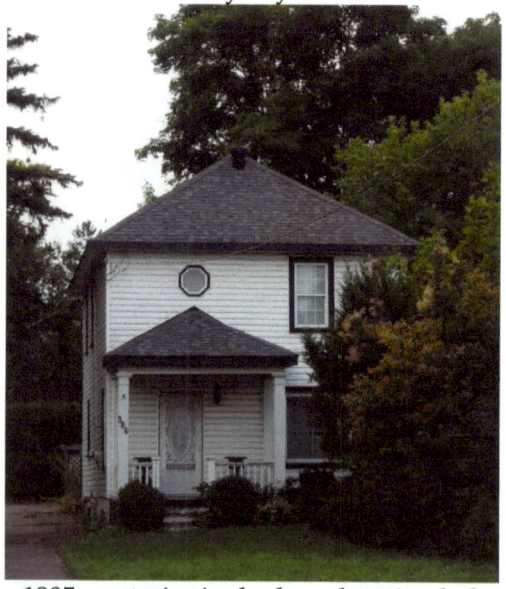

386 King Street – 1905 – exterior is clapboard; stained glass fanlight above front window; hipped roof; second storey octagonal window

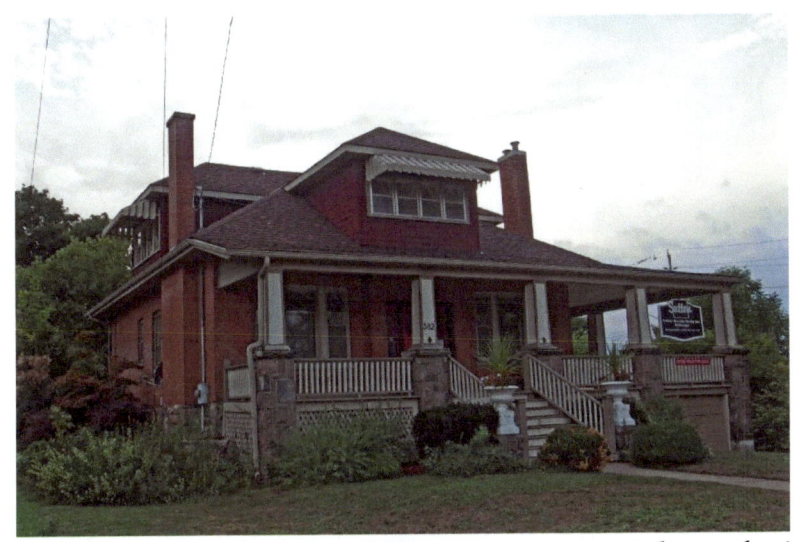

382 King Street - Craighead House - cottage style roof with four widows' watch dormers; large two-sided porch supported with cut stone columns, open railing; brick exterior; bay windows

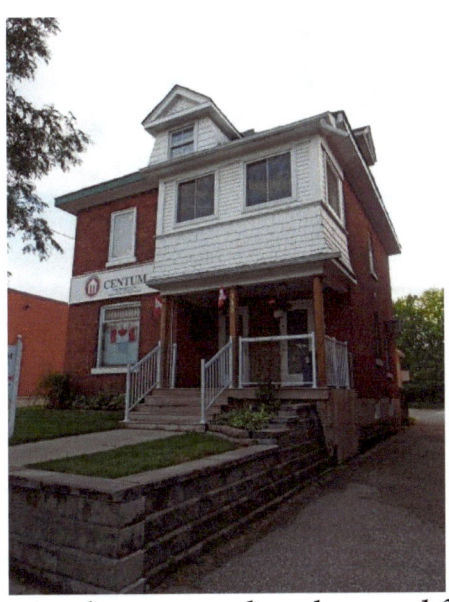

348 King Street – dormer; enclosed second floor balcony

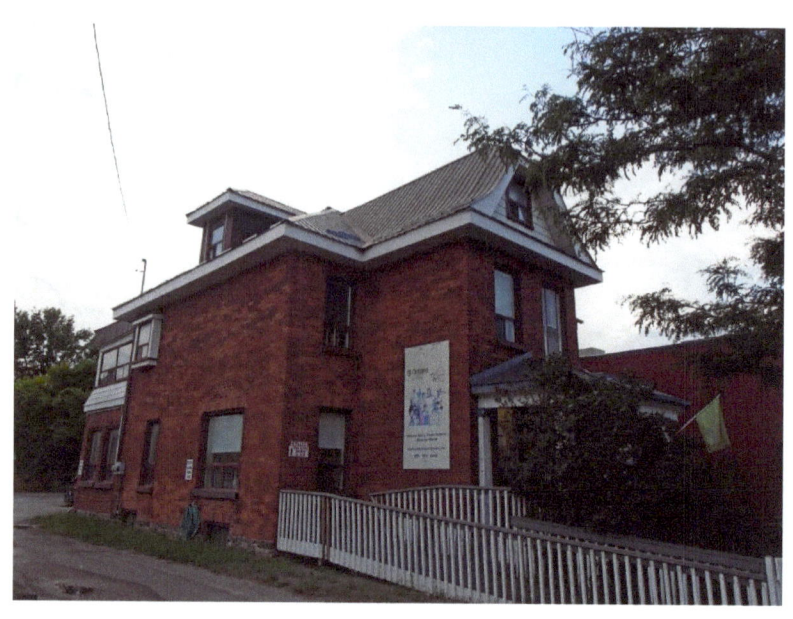

356 King Street

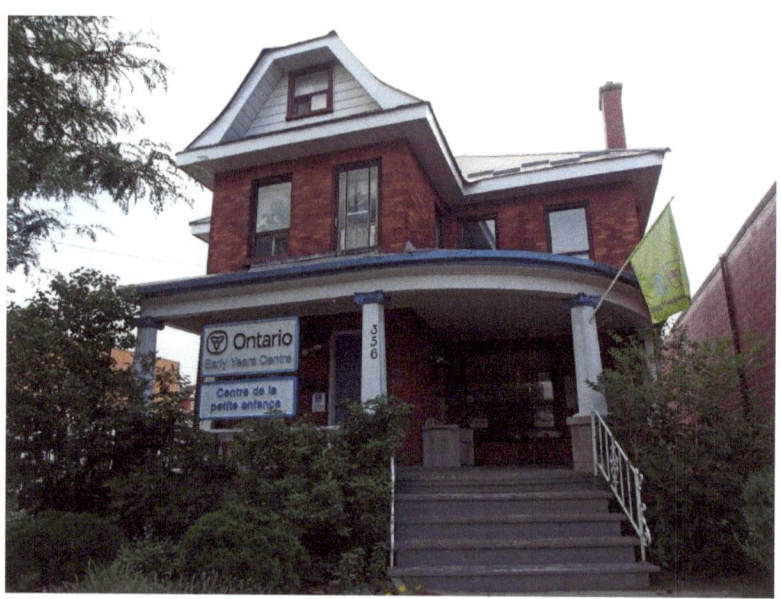

Wraparound verandah

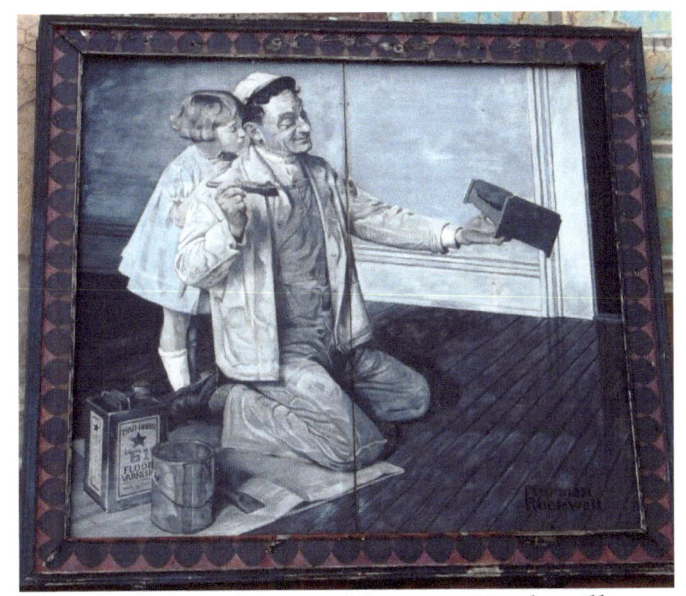

A Day for Mary – Norman Rockwell

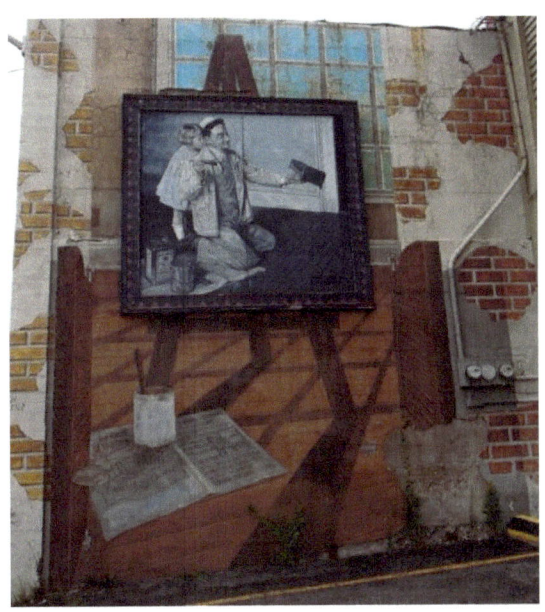

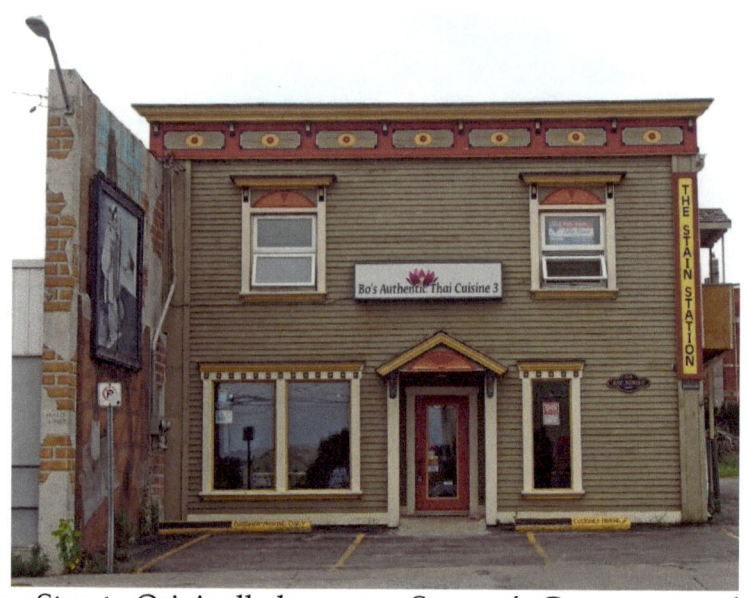

555 Bay Street - Originally known as Stewart's Garage - stored cars for island cottagers. This single detached, two storey building has a flat roof. The exterior is finished with clapboard. The windows have a flat opening with an entablature and a blind transom on the upper storey windows with a molded lug sill, and decorated headers with molded lug sills on the first storey. The main entrance is located at the center of the façade and there is a plain pediment above the door. There is also flat trim around the opening.

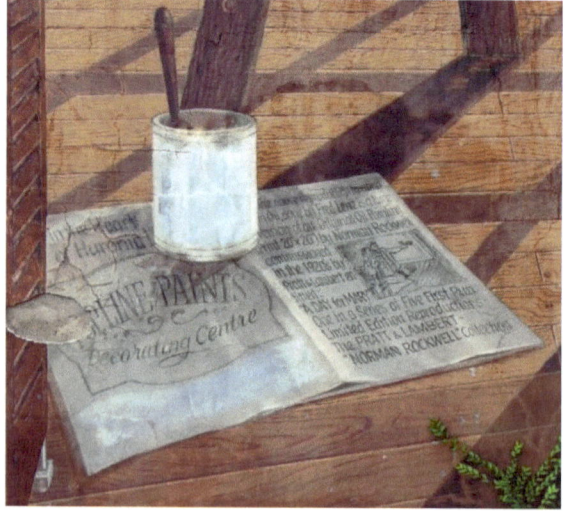

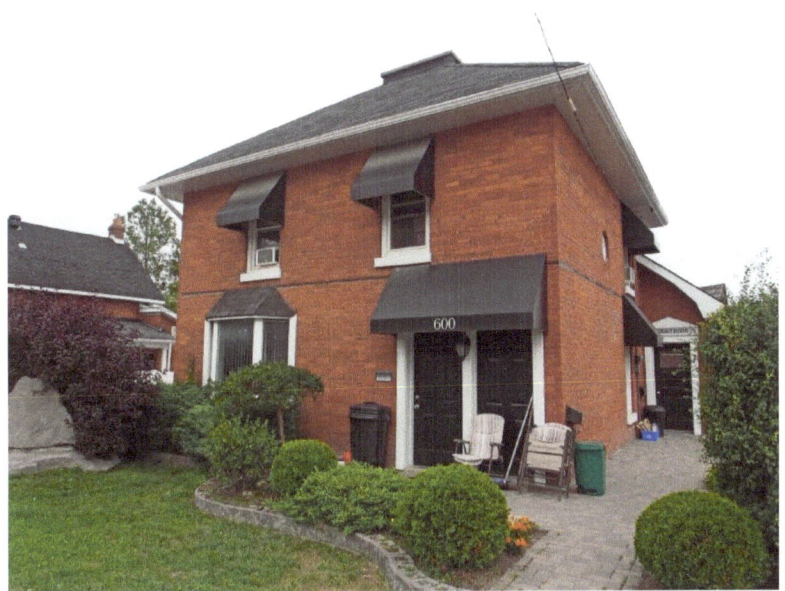

600 Bay Street - built in 1904 - truncated pyramidal roof; the exterior of the house is finished with stretcher brick. The windows have a flat opening with a plain lug sill; bay window; pediment above the double door

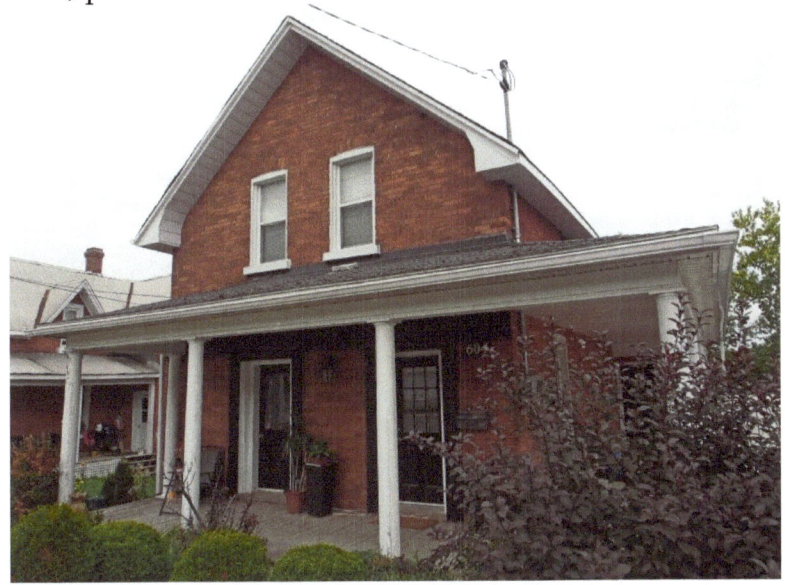

604 Bay Street – Gothic – gabled roof; columns with Doric capitals supporting wraparound veranda

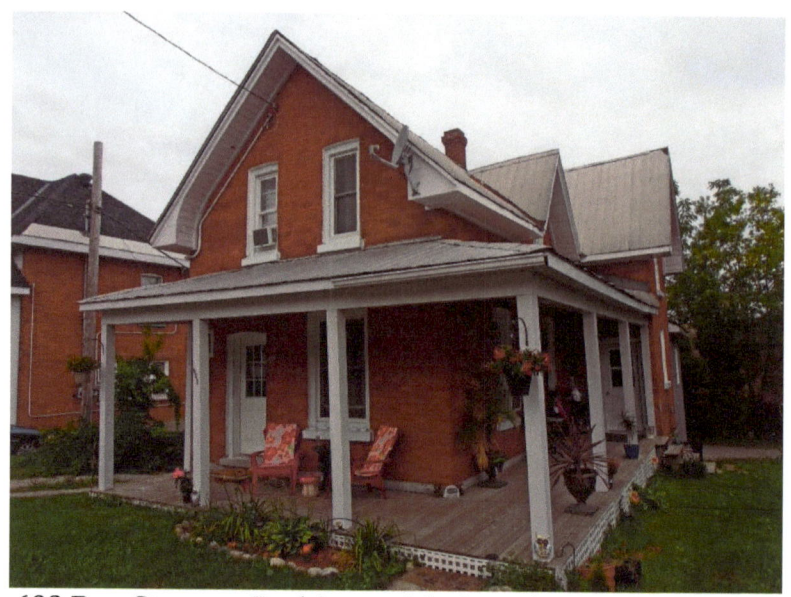

608 Bay Street – Gothic – gabled roof; square columns supporting wraparound verandah roof

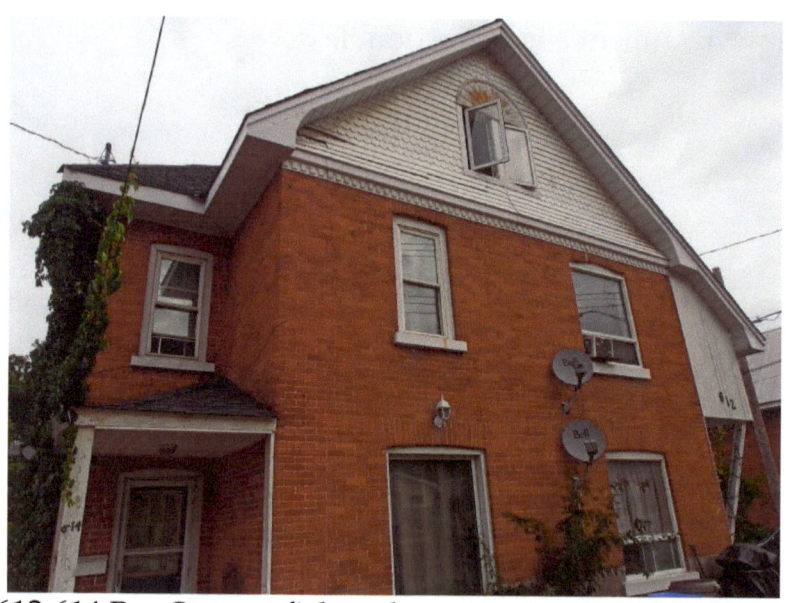

612-614 Bay Street – fish scale patterning in gable, dentil molding

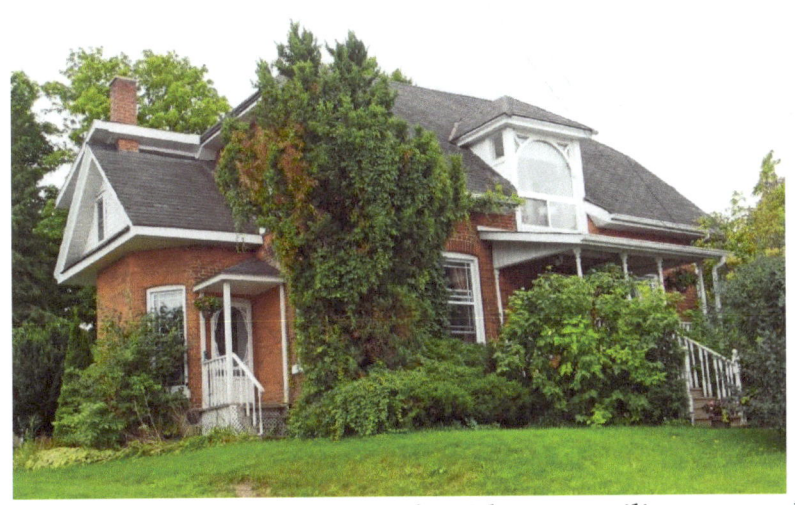

615 Bay Street – dormers, porch with open railing; veranda
with wood-turned columns and open railing; voussoirs

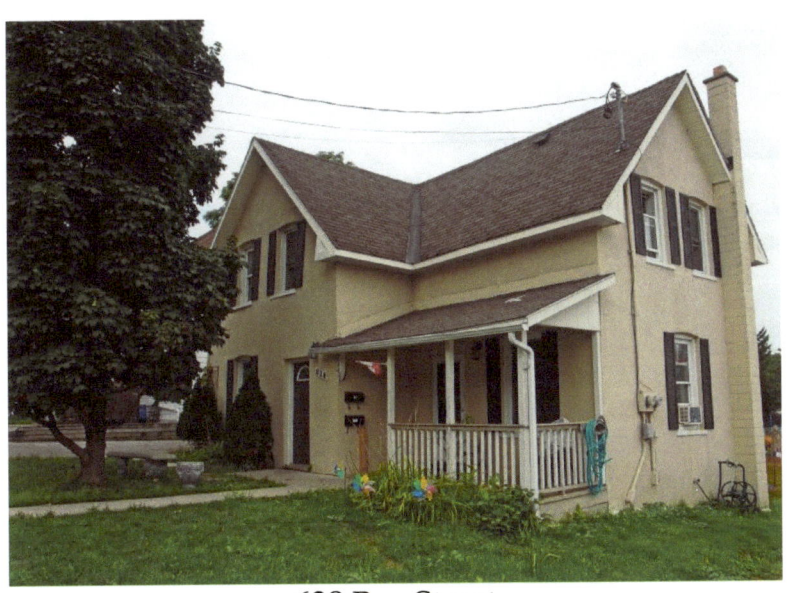

638 Bay Street

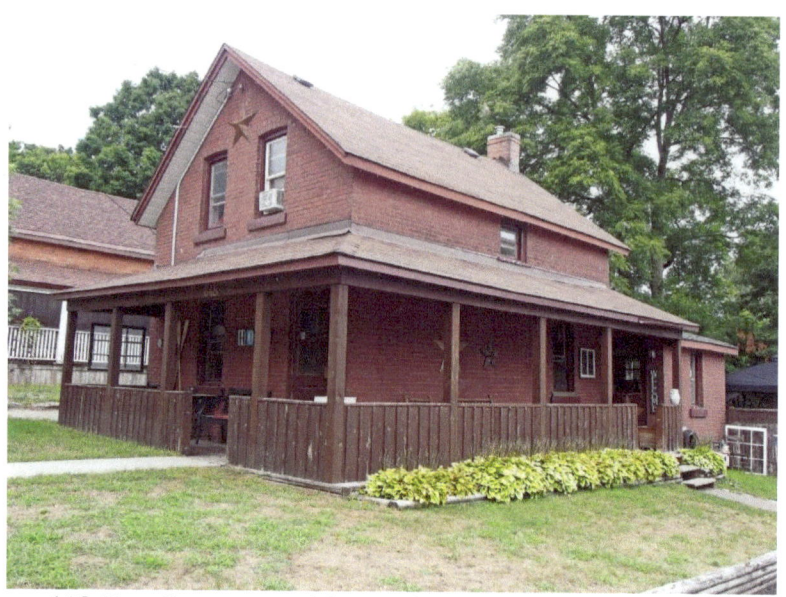

648 Bay Street – gable roof, wraparound veranda

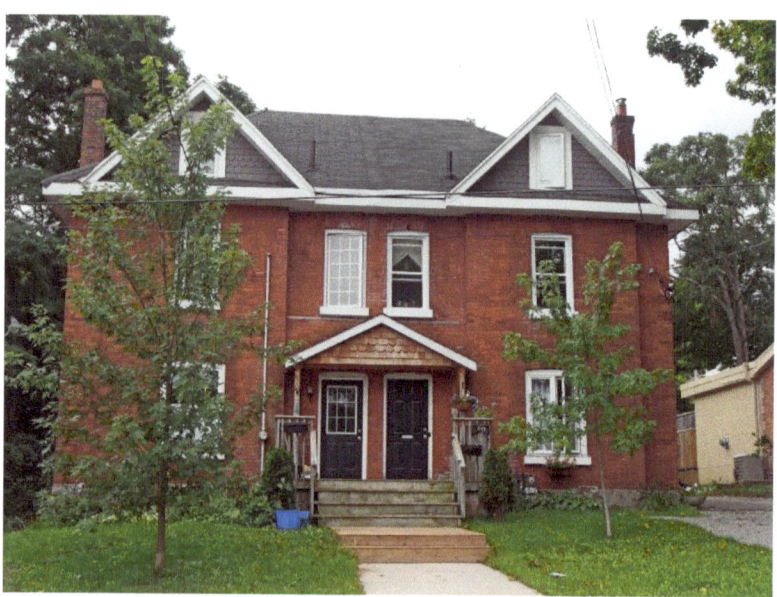

647-649 Bay Street - gable roofed dormers; cedar shingles in open pediment above doors

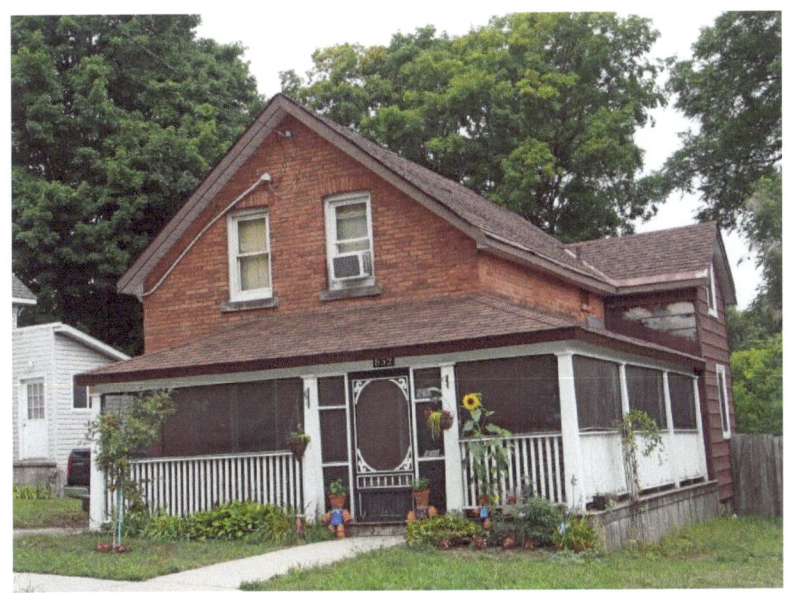

652 Bay Street

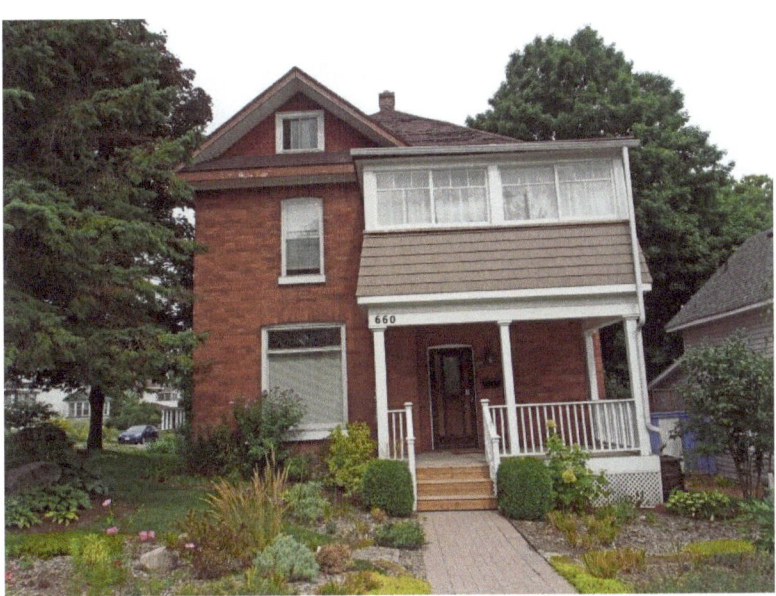

660 Bay Street - gable roofed dormers; enclosed second floor
balcony above open veranda supported by square pillars,
open railing; stained glass window

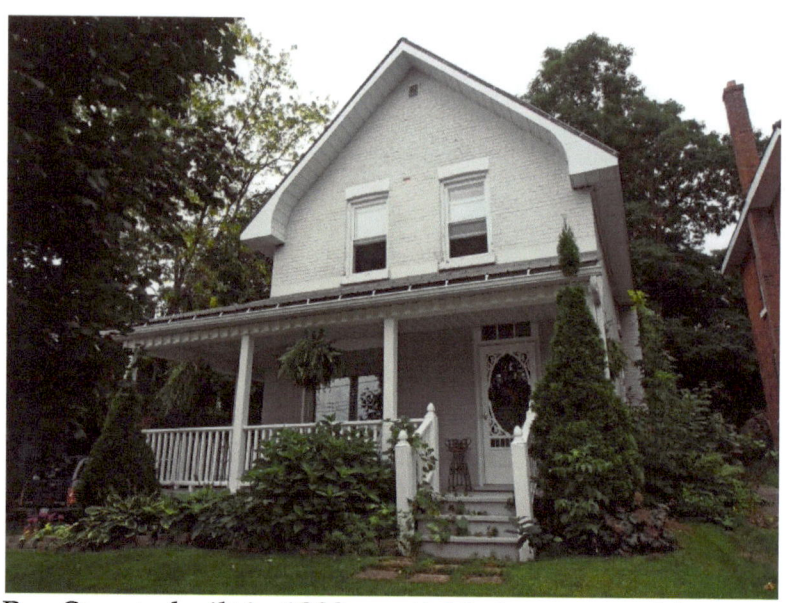

645 Bay Street - built in 1890, partial below ground basement; stretcher brick exterior; medium gable steel roof with a projecting eaves gable dormer on side of house; windows with brick voussoirs and a plain lug sill; multi-light transom window; porch has an open railing with wood piers

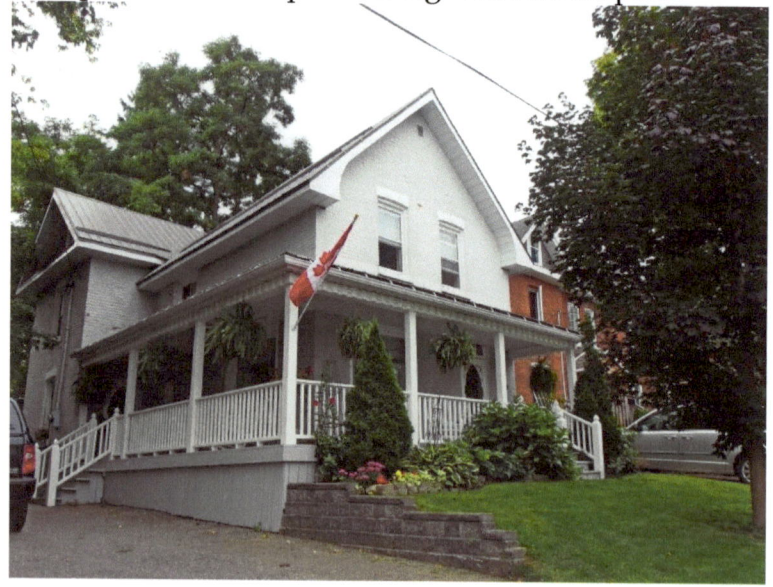

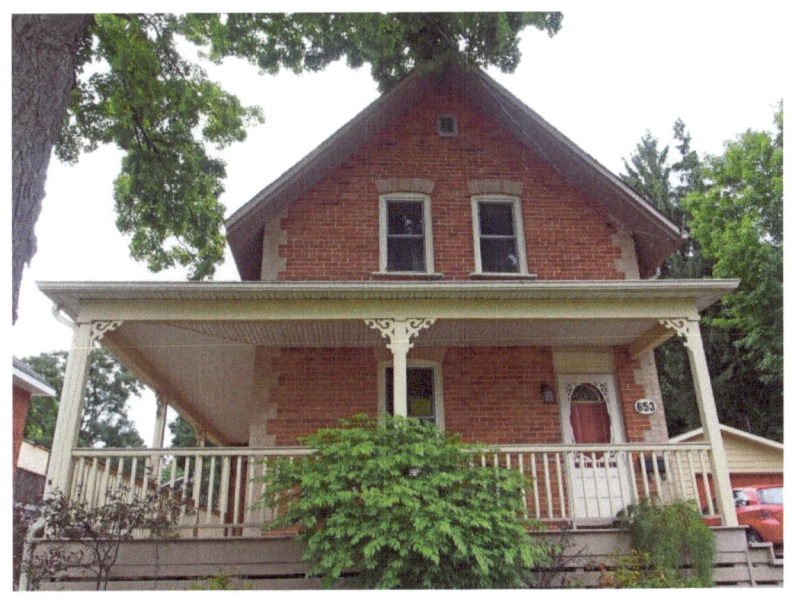

653 Bay Street – Gothic – voussoirs; decorative support posts
for verandah, open railing; corner quoins

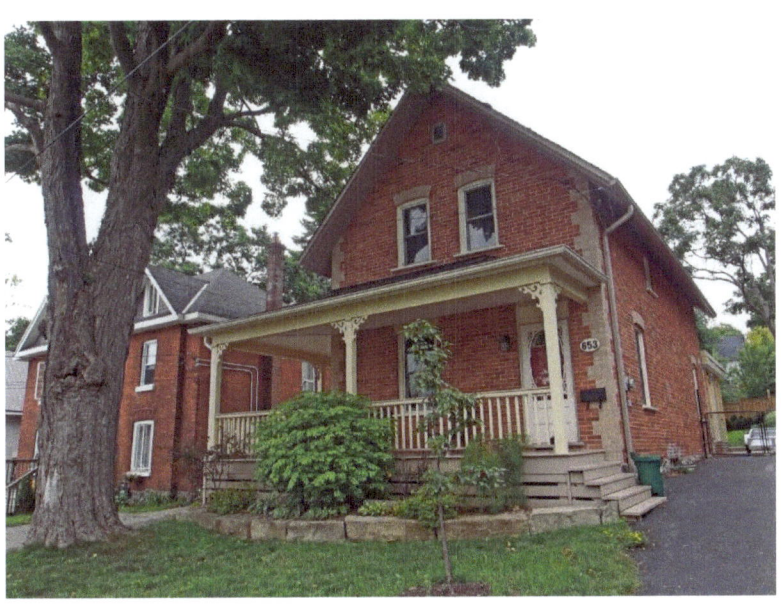

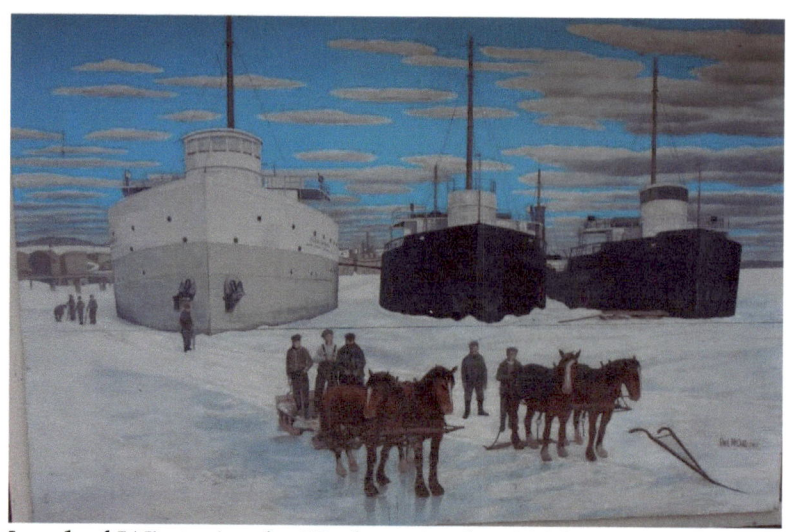

Mural of *Winter at the Harbour* in the 1920s and 1930s. The workhorses were used to break the ice so that the ships could come closer to shore.

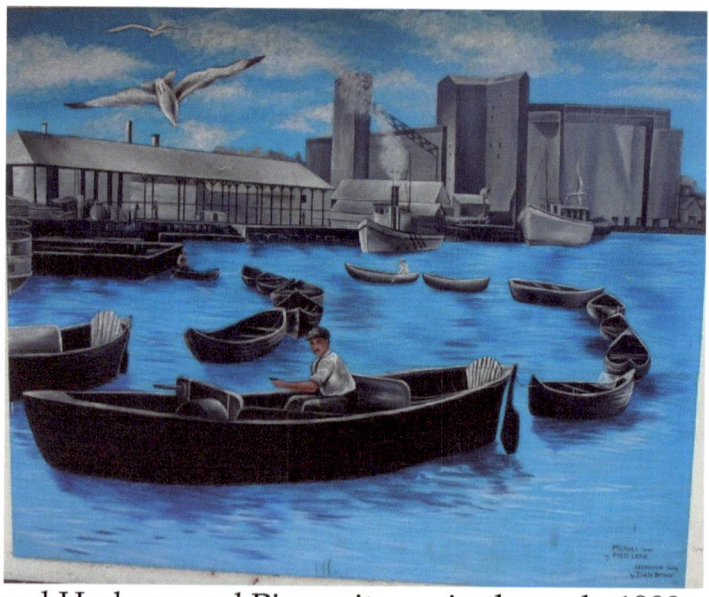

Midland Harbour and Pier as it was in the early 1900s. This was the last mural Fred Lenz painted before he passed away.

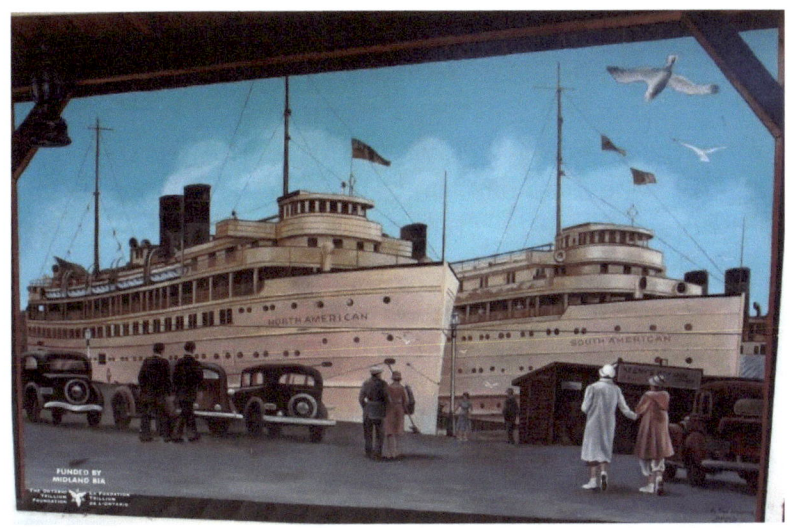

Great Lake Cruises - These two ships belonged to the Detroit based Georgian Bay Lines. The ships picked passengers up from Great Lake cities and transported them to quiet picturesque waters.

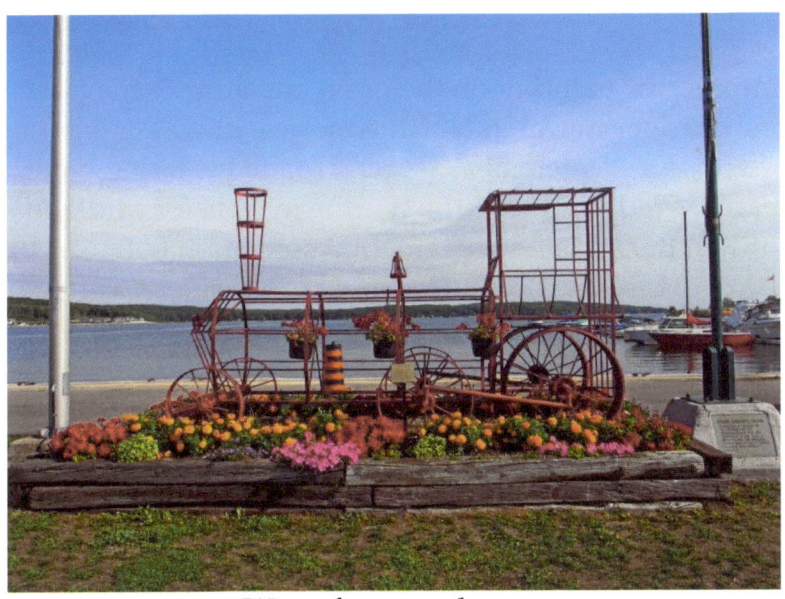

Waterfront sculpture

We travel through life, Sometimes much too fast,
Looking for things that will surely last,
A beautiful sky, a majestic tree,
But nothing permanent for you and me
Perhaps someone to love, such as family or friend,
But they too pass on to their eventual end.
But hopefully not all these loving memories are gone
Surely loving memories linger on and on.
So as we travel through life, much too fast,
These lovely memories are the things that will last and last.
By Dr. Kenneth S. Lewis, Midland, July 2011

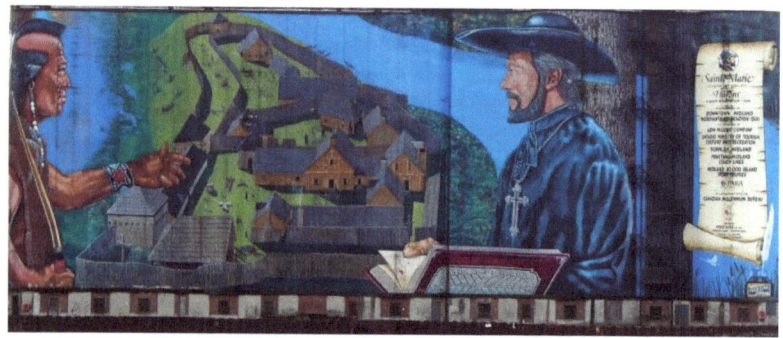

The impressive painting on the grain elevators is the largest
historic outdoor mural in North America. It was created by
Fred Lenz. A commercial artist who made his living painting
billboards, Fred produced thirty-nine murals for Midland's
downtown Business Improvement Association between 1991
and 2000, and several private murals for businesses and
individuals. Fred began the painting on the elevators in 1999
as a Millennium project. The mural features a Huron man
meeting a Jesuit missionary, with an aerial view of Sainte-
Marie among the Hurons between them. The work measures
24 x 60 metres (80 x 200 feet). Fred died of cancer in 2001
before the elevator mural was finished. Michele van Maurik,
Fred's sons, and other artists finished the mural that Fred
described as "the pinnacle of my life in art".

Trumpeter Swan Sculpture
- designed and sculpted by Ron Hunt

Centuries ago these skies and local wetlands were home to North America's largest waterfowl, the majestic Trumpeter Swan. Trumpeter Swans are named for their distinctive bugling call as a result of a loop in the bird's larynx. Weighing 9-12 kilograms - with a wingspan nearly three meters, trumpeters can fly up to 35 kilometers per hour. They feed on aquatic vegetation and wild grasses and live as long as twenty years in the wild.

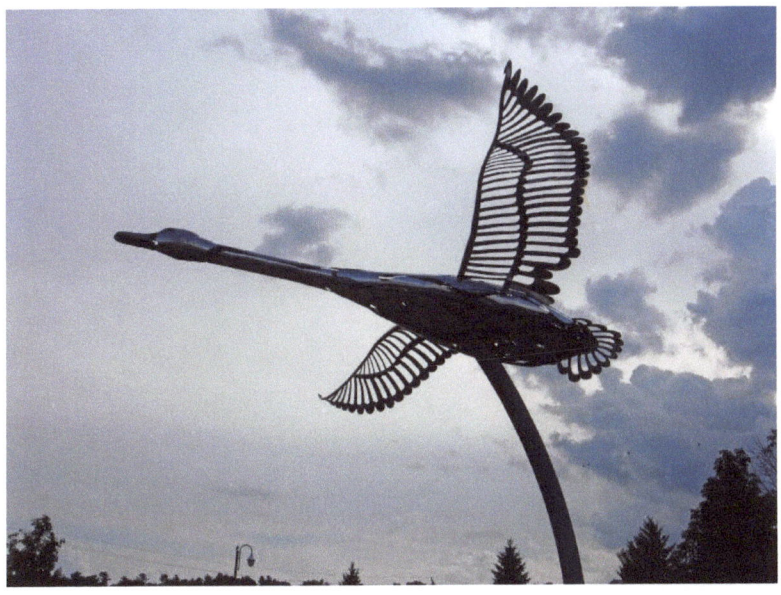

Valued for their meat, skin and feathers, Trumpeter Swans were over-hunted and by 1933 there were only 77 birds breeding in all of Canada. The species was further threatened by destruction of their wetland environment. *Cygnus buccinator* was designated as an endangered species until 1984. It is now considered a Protected Species in Ontario, making it illegal to hunt or harass them.

Midland's Wye Marsh began a re-introduction program in 1988 with one breeding pair. Today the Marsh cares for and monitors about one-third of Ontario's Trumpeter Swan population. Despite good care and feeding, the species faces threats from raptors, snapping turtles, mink, coyotes, foxes, raccoons and disease. Despite a national ban on lead shot, poisoning continues to be a major obstacle to the health and survival of the swans.

This stainless steel sculpture represents the signature program of the Wye Marsh and stands as a tribute to the volunteers, donors, individuals and corporations, who support the environmental programs of the Wye Marsh Wildlife Center.

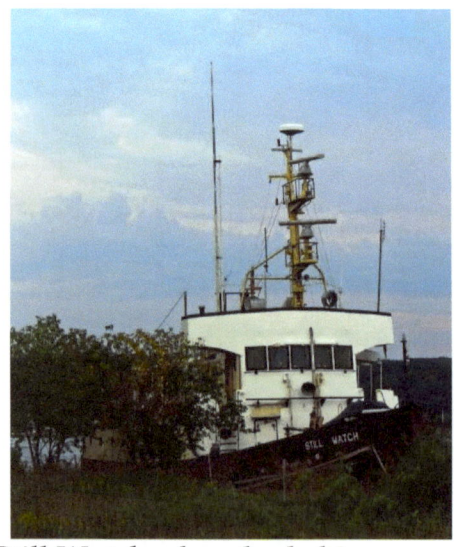
Still Watch – beached ship

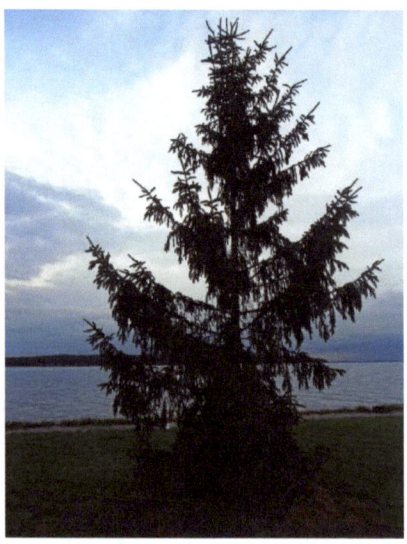
Tree silhouetted at sunset

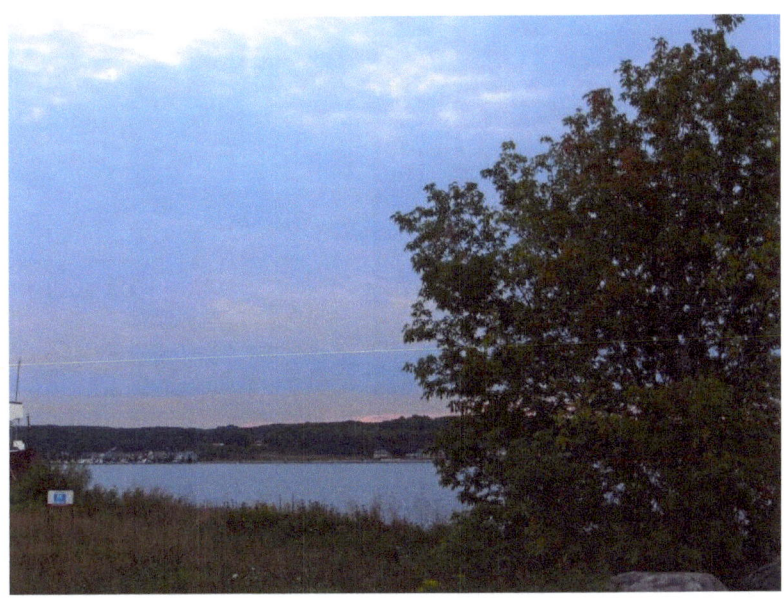

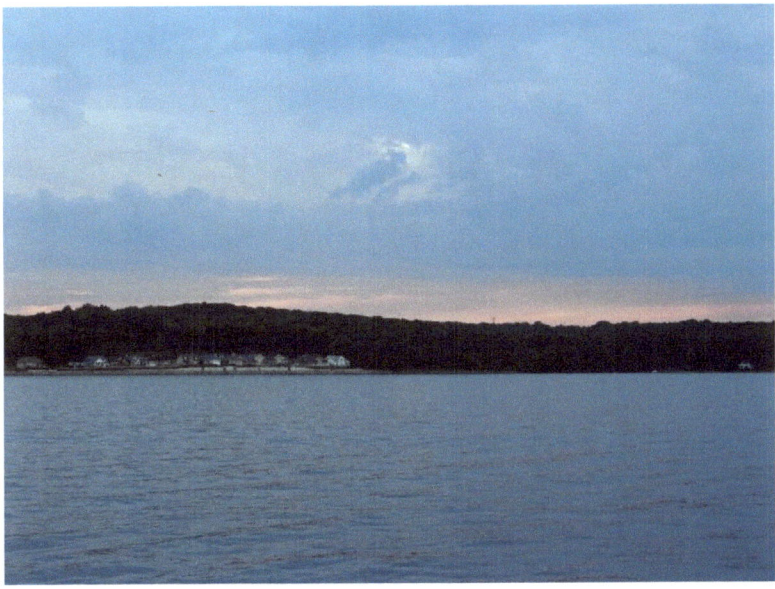

Sainte-Marie among the Hurons

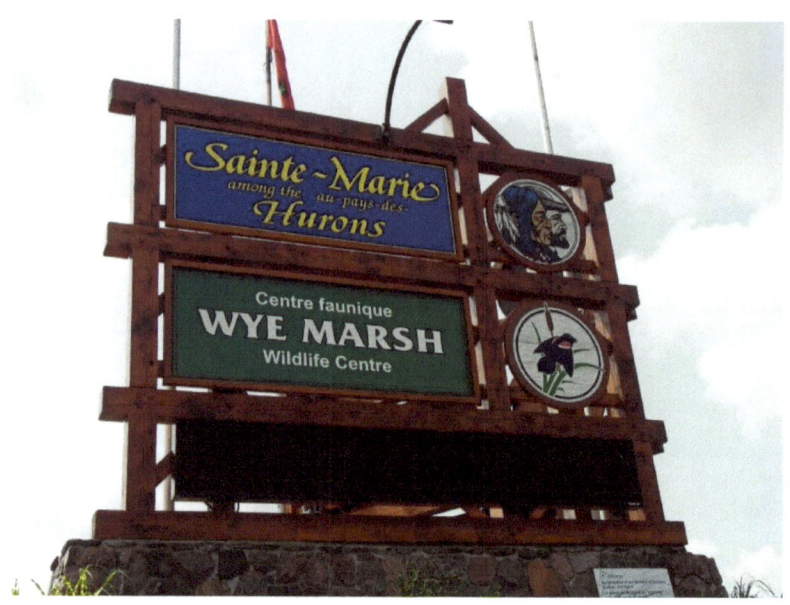

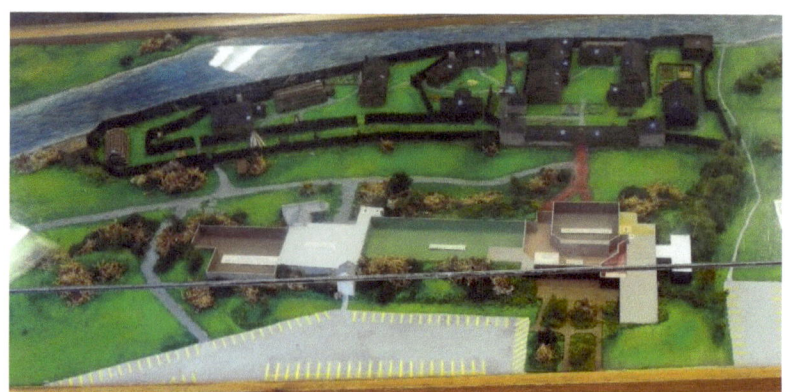

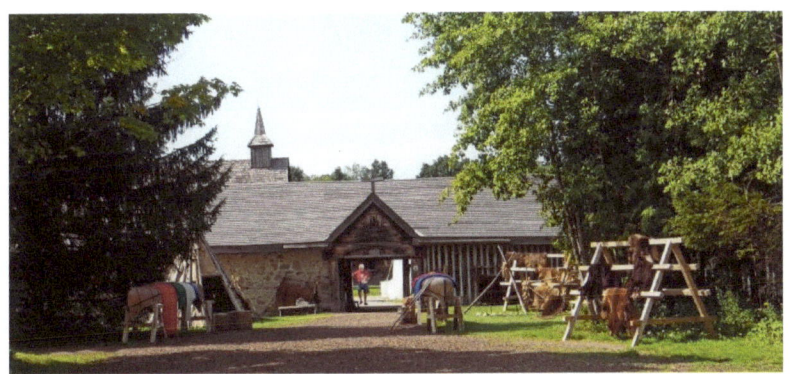

The French supplemented their agricultural efforts with fish and wild game, and then used the furs and hides.

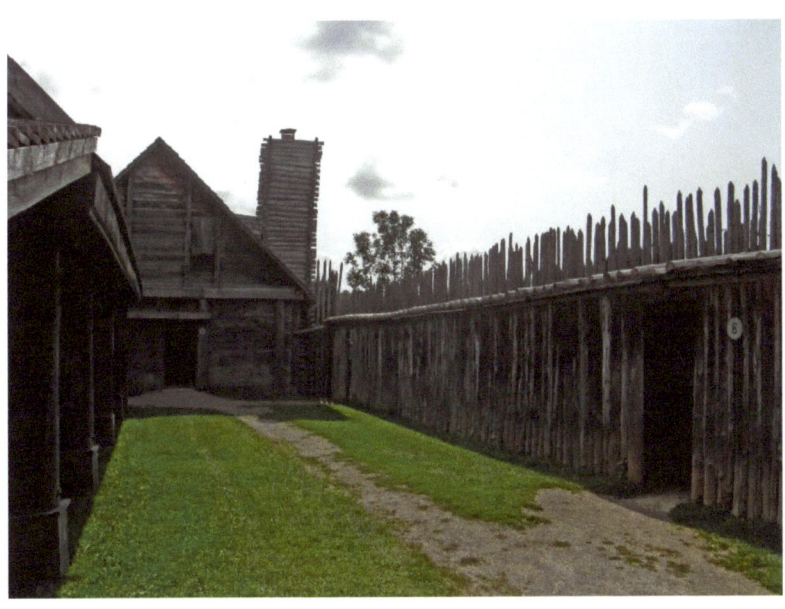

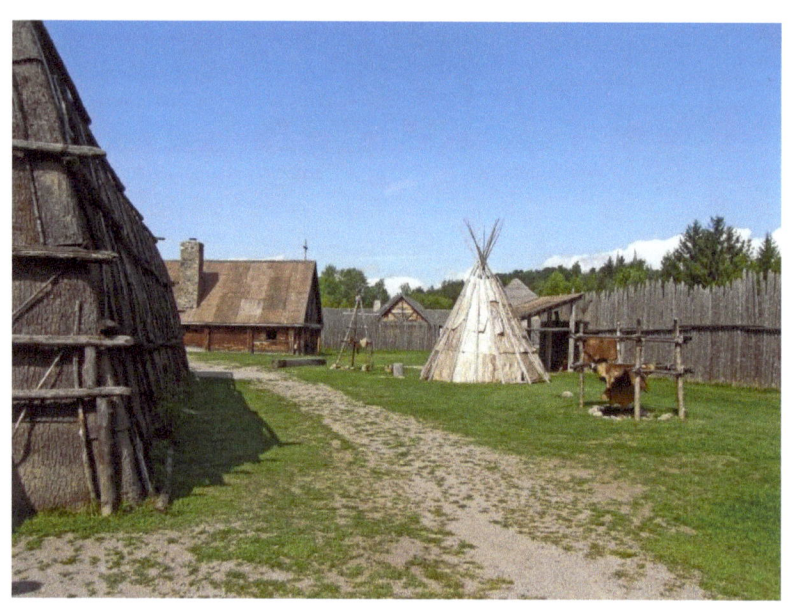

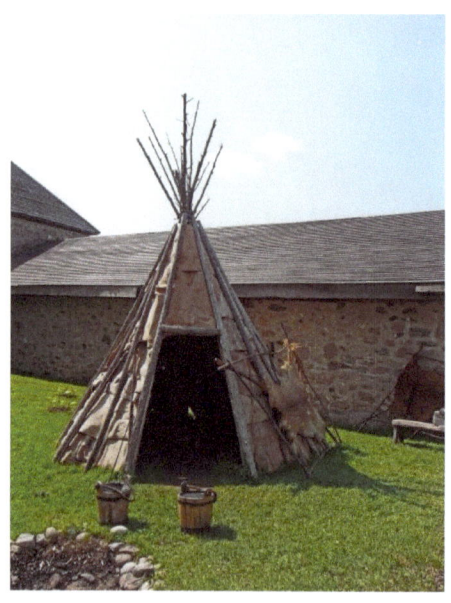

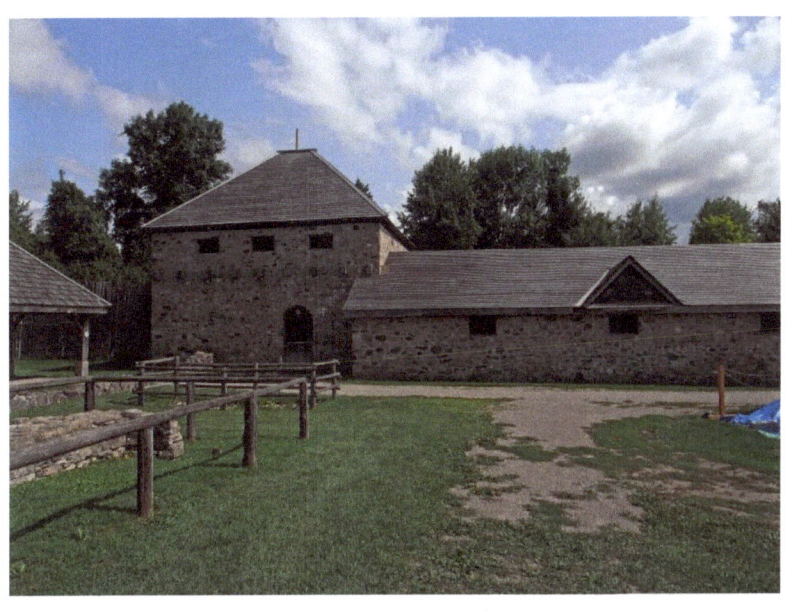

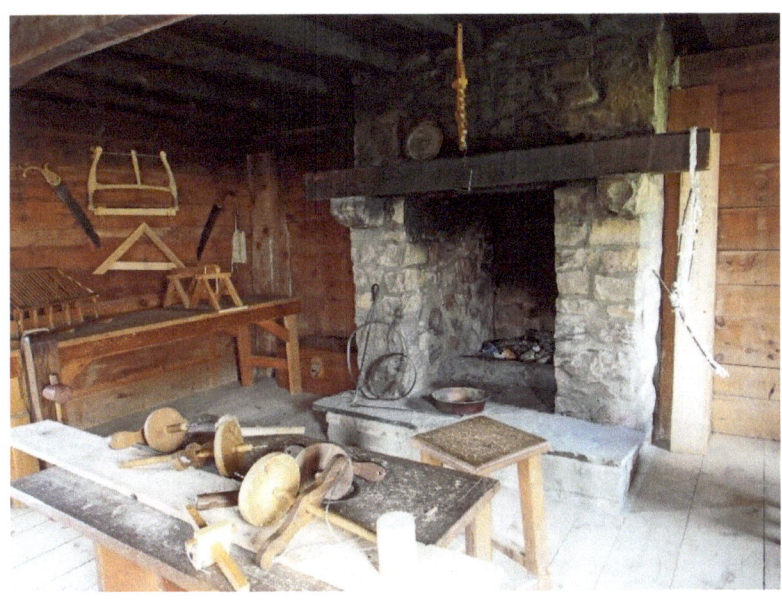

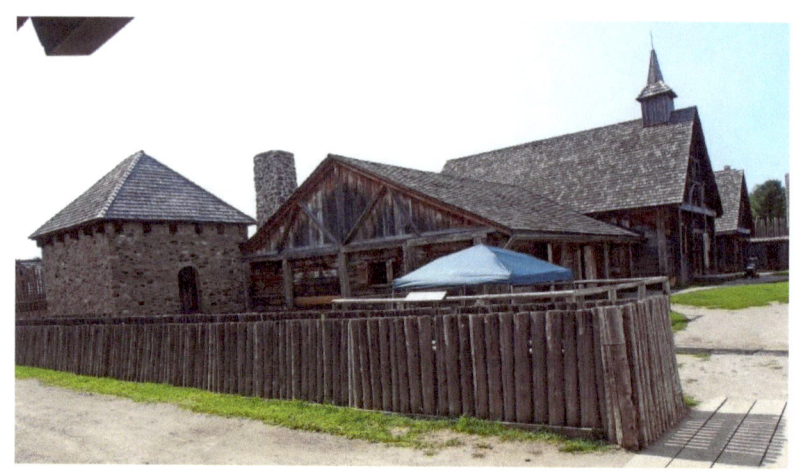

Church of St. Joseph in background

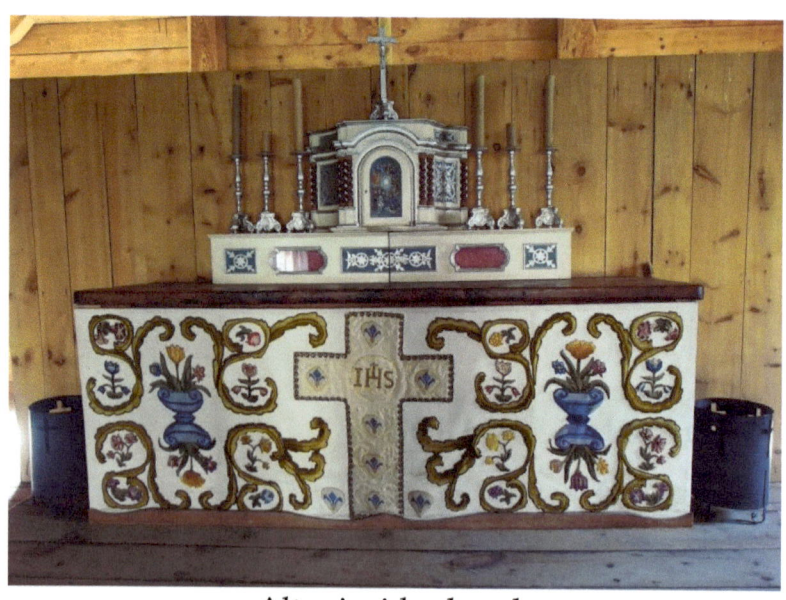

Altar inside church

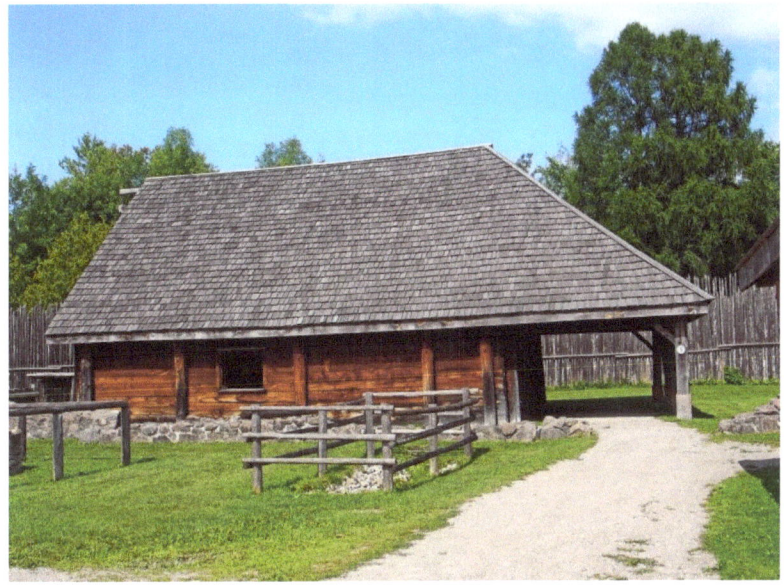

The Granary – The establishment of farming operations provided the community with a stable food supply.

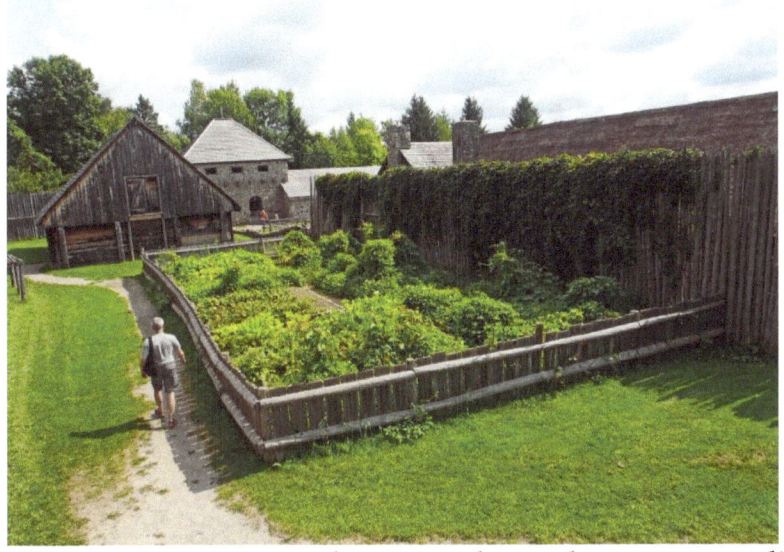

Carrots, beets, turnips and peas made meals more appealing to the French who were unaccustomed to a diet consisting mainly of corn.

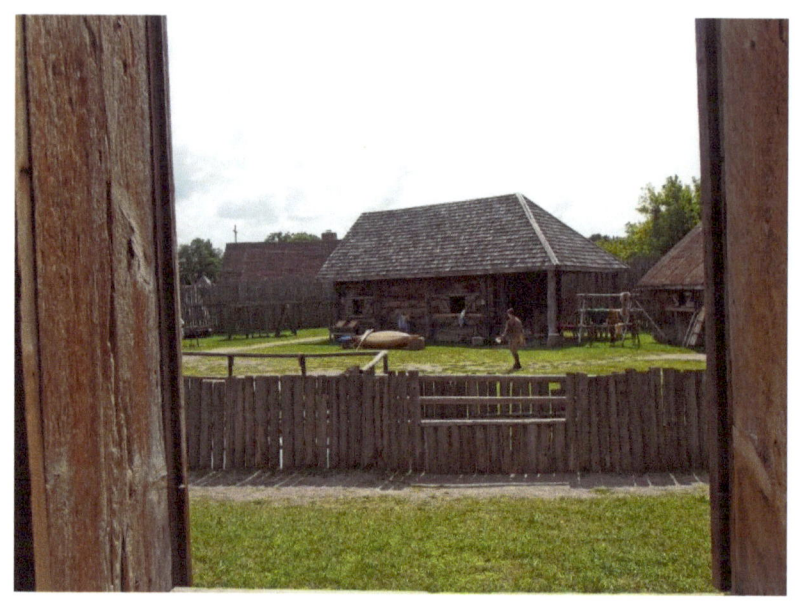

Shoemaker/Tailor Shop – Fabrics sent from France were sewn into clothing.

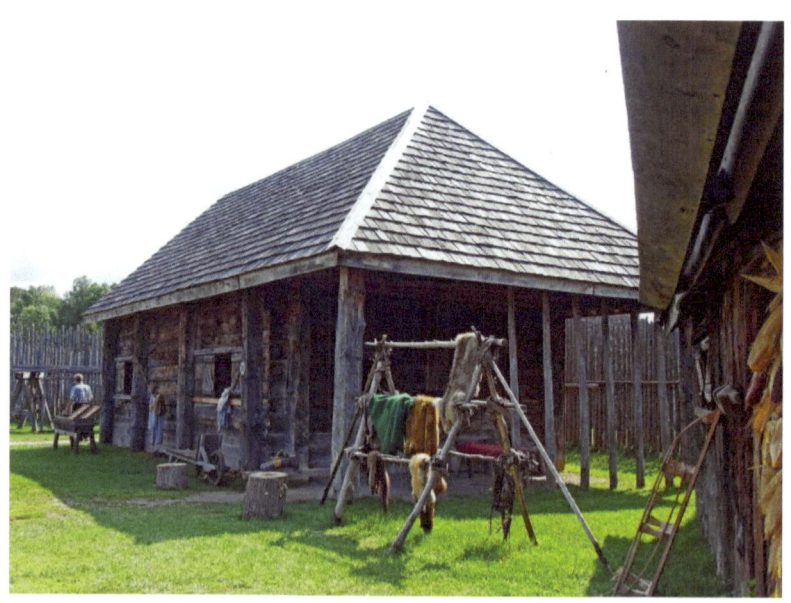

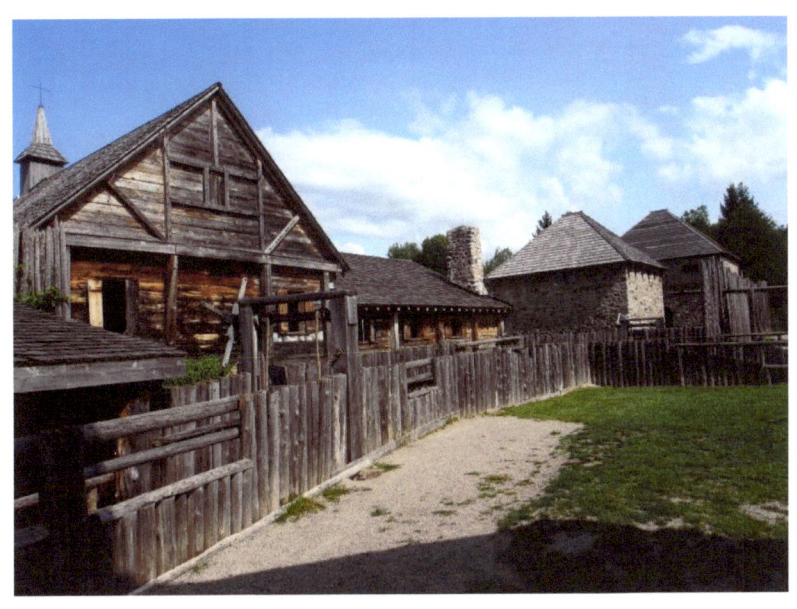

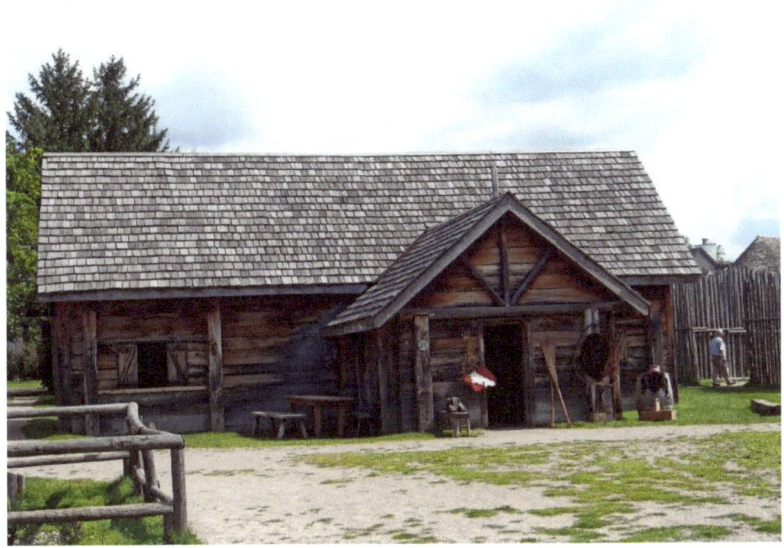

Supply Depot

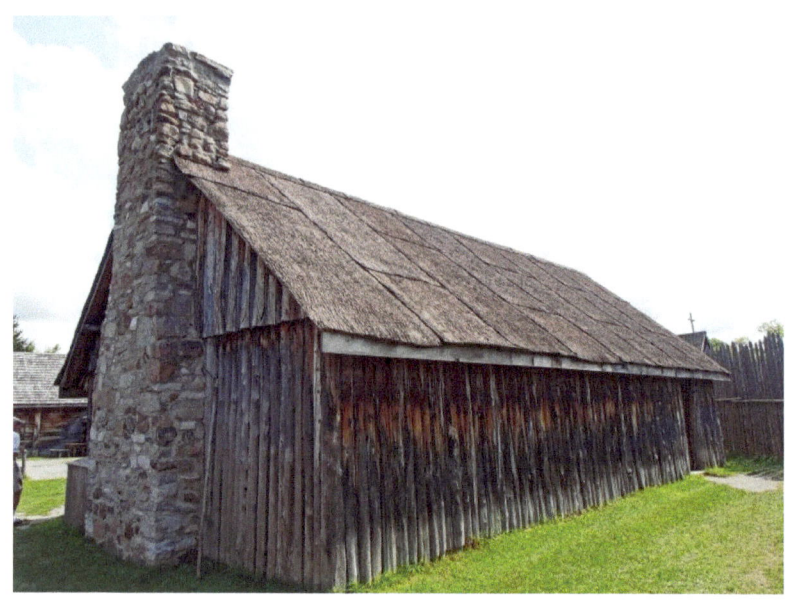

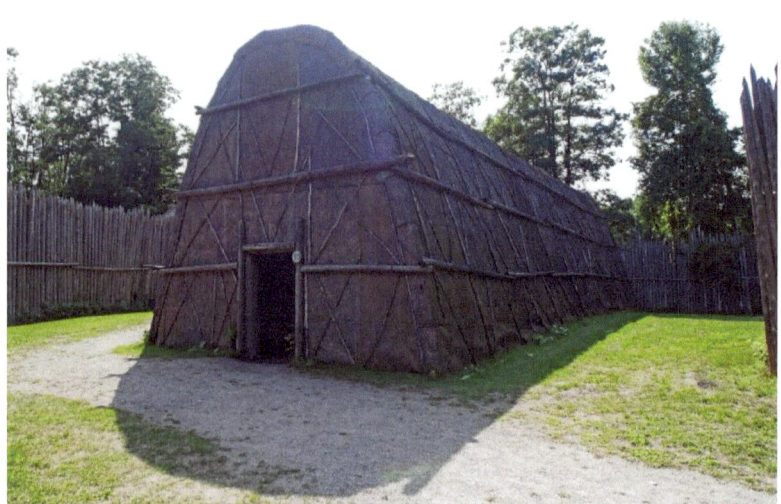

Longhouse like those found in Wendat (Huron) villages

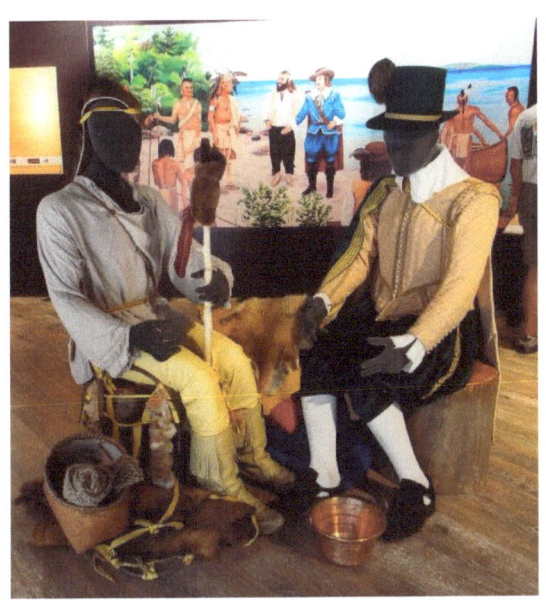

Champlain travelled with two Frenchmen and ten Wendat in two canoes from Lachine Rapids on July 8, 1615. They went up the Ottawa River, through Lake Nipissing, down the French River and arrived at Lake Huron on July 29. They paddled south along Georgian Bay about 180 kilometers and arrived in Huronia; they then walked to several villages, staying in the area for ten months. Champlain noted that the Hurons traded corn and fishnets for furs with Algonquin groups, and for tobacco from other groups.

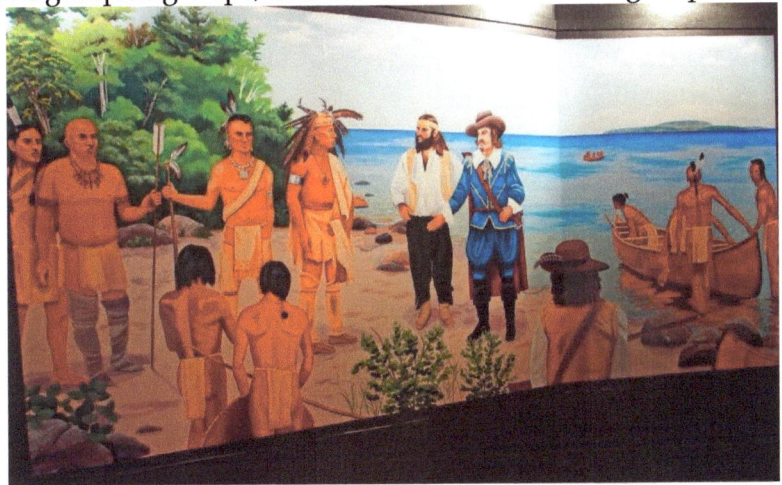

Architectural Terms

Bay Window: A window that projects out from a wall, in a semicircular, rectangular, or polygonal design. Used frequently in Gothic and Victorian designs. Example: 409 King Street, Page 33	
Capital: The uppermost finish or decoration on a column. A Doric column is characterized by a plain column with no base, a shaft with twenty flutings, and a simple capital with a simple entablature. Example: 408 King Street, Page 33	
Cobblestone architecture: Refers to the use of cobblestones embedded in mortar as a method for erecting walls on houses and commercial buildings. Example: King Street – field stone walls, and cobblestone basement, Page 28	
Course: continuous horizontal row or layer of stone or brick. Example: 320 King Street, Page 7	
Dentil Moulding: an even series of rectangles used as ornamental decoration in cornices. Example: 262 King Street, Page 12	
Dichromatic brickwork: the use of two colours of brick, tile or slate to decorate a façade. Example: 486 Bay Street, Page 24	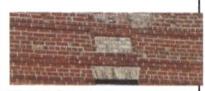

Dormer: (French for "sleep") a gable end window that pierces through the plane of a sloping roof surface to create usable space in the top floor or attic of a building by adding headroom. Example: 414 King Street, Page 32	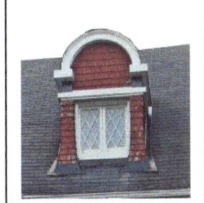
Frontispiece: a portion of the façade of a building, usually a centred doorway that is slightly raised from the rest of the building, usually has extensive ornamentation. Frontispieces are usually Classical in design with white columned porches. Example: 203-207 King Street, Page 19	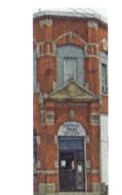
Gable: the triangular portion of a wall between the edges of a sloping roof. Example: 431 King Street, Page 31	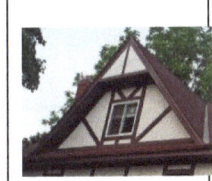
Gambrel Roof: a symmetrical two-sided roof with two slopes on each side; the upper slope is positioned at a shallow angle, while the lower slope is steep. It is similar to a mansard roof, but a gambrel has vertical gable ends instead of being hipped at the four corners of the building. Example: King Street, Page 28	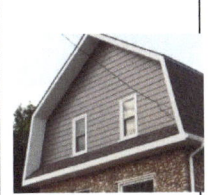
Hipped Roof: a roof where all sides slope downwards to the walls with no gables. Example: 687 King Street, Page 26	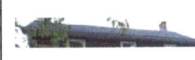

Keystones and Voussoirs: a voussoir is a wedge-shaped element used in building an arch. A keystone is the central stone that locks all the stones into position, allowing the arch to bear weight. A keystone is often enlarged and embellished. Example: 203-207 King Street, Page 19	
Mansard Roof: This style was popularized by Francois Mansart (1598-1666), an accomplished architect of the French Baroque period and especially fashionable during the Second French Empire (1852-1870). This roof is almost flat on the top section, with two slopes on each of its sides with the lower slope at a steeper angle than the upper and having dormer windows. Example: 213-219 King Street, Page 23	
Palladian Window: a large window that is divided into three sections with the centre section larger than the two side sections and usually arched. Example: 409 King Street, Page 33	
Pediment: a triangular section above the door or portico, usually supported by columns. The inside of the triangle is called the tympanum. Example: 647-649 Bay Street, Page 44	
Pilaster: a slightly projecting column built into or applied to the face of a wall for additional structural support. Example: 251 King Street, Page 12	

Quoin: masonry blocks at the corner of a wall, often a decorative feature, usually larger or of a different colour than the rest of the wall. Example: 234-236 King Street, Page 14	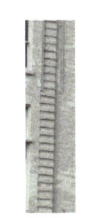
Sidelight: a vertical window that flanks a door, and is often used to emphasize the importance of a primary entrance. Example: 687 King Street, Page 26	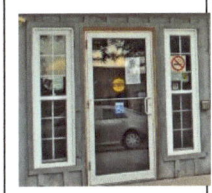
Tower: A circular, square, or octagonal vertical structure higher than the surrounding structure that is usually part of an existing building and is created either for extra defense or for a specific purpose such as a clock or a bell tower. Example: 320 King Street, Page 6	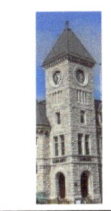
Transom Window: the light above the doorway, also called a fanlight. Example: 645 Bay Street, Page 47	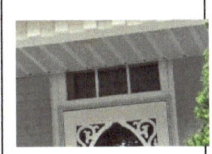
Verge board and Finial: also called bargeboards – hang from the projecting end of a roof and are often elaborately carved and ornamented. **Finial:** ornament added to the top of a gable, pinnacle, canopy or spire – a Gothic element. Example: 414 King Street, Page 32	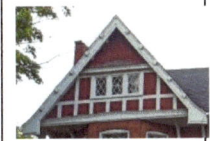

Georgian, before 1860 – This style began with the British King Georges in the 18th century. These buildings have balanced facades around a central door, medium-pitched gable roofs, and small paned windows. Example: 400 King Street, Page 34	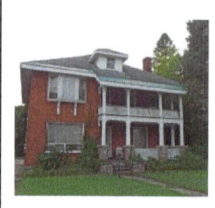
Gothic Revival, 1830-1890 – These decorative buildings have sharply-pitched gables with highly detailed verge boards, pointed-arch window openings, and dichromatic brickwork. It is a common style in Ontario. Example: 414 King Street, Page 32	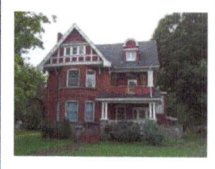
Italianate, 1850-1900 – A two story rectangular building with a mild hip roof, a projecting frontispiece, and generous eaves with ornate cornice brackets was the basis of the style; often there are large sash windows, quoins, ornate detailing on the windows, belvederes and wraparound verandahs. Italianate commercial buildings often have cast iron cresting and elegant window surrounds. Example: 472 King Street – entrance, Page 30	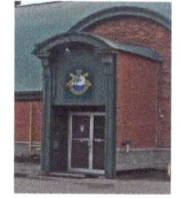

A **log cabin**, built from logs, was usually one- or 1½-storeys constructed with round rather than hewn, or hand-worked, logs, and erected quickly for frontier shelter. Log cabins were built from logs laid horizontally and interlocked on the ends with notches. The cabin was situated to provide sunlight and drainage so the pioneers could cope better with the rigors of frontier life. The pioneers chose old-growth trees that were straight and had few knots and did not need to be hewn to fit well together. Careful notching minimized the size of the gap between the logs and reduced the amount of chinking with sticks and rocks or daubing with mud to fill the gap. The length of one log was the length of one wall.

Example: 687 King Street, Page 26

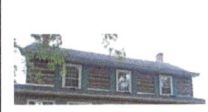

Neo-colonial (also Colonial Revival, Georgian Revival or Neo-Georgian) architecture seeks to revive elements of architectural style of American colonial architecture of the period around the Revolutionary War which drew strongly from Georgian architecture of Great Britain. Architecture from the 18th and early 19th centuries in Ontario includes a wide assortment of detailing and ornament applied to a design centered around the fireplace and the source of water. Structures are typically two stories, have a symmetrical front facade with elaborate front doorways, often with decorative crown pediments, fanlights, and sidelights, symmetrical windows flanking the front entrance, often in pairs or threes, and columned porches. Example: King Street, Page 28	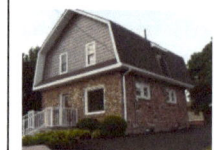
Romanesque Revival, 1880-1910 – This style hearkens back to medieval architecture of the 11th and 12th centuries with a heavy appearance, blocky towers and rounded arches. Example: 320 King Street, Page 6	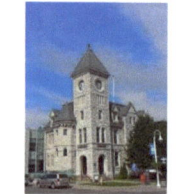
Second Empire, 1860-1880 – The mansard roof is the most noteworthy feature of this style and is evidence of the French origins. Projecting central towers and one or two-storey bays can also be present. Example: 213-219 King Street, Page 23	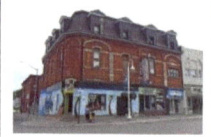